How to Sell Yourself as an Actor

(from New York to Los Angeles and everywhere in between)

by

K Callan

second edition/completely revised

Sweden Press
Box 1612
Studio City, CA 91614

Other books by K Callan

The Los Angeles Agent Book.1 (The Actor's Workbook) 1986
The New York Agent Book, 1987
The Los Angeles Agent Book.2 1988
The New York Agent Book.2 1990
The Los Angeles Agent Book.3 1990
The Life of the Party 1991
The Los Angeles Agent Book.4 1992

Cover: Katie Maratta
Cover design: Devine Design

ISBN 0-9617336-7-5
Library of Congress Catalog Card Number 91-65952

Acknowledgement

As usual, books don't happen by themselves. Or even by myself. Thank you Jeff Rose and Kristi Callan for copy editing. Thank you Adele Weitz for continuing computer support and David Nolte for design and paste-ups.

Dedication

Gwen Feldman of Samuel French in Los Angeles asked me to write a book about the business that would be helpful to actors everywhere. That's how *How to Sell Yourself as an Actor* came into existence back in 1988 and I happily dedicated that book to her.

This new edition comes about because times change and new data in the form of information and experience has become available. I would like to dedicate this edition to all the people who keep educating me about the business: my fellow actors, directors, producers, writers, agents as well as readers who have called or written posing questions or sharing experiences that enriched my thought process.

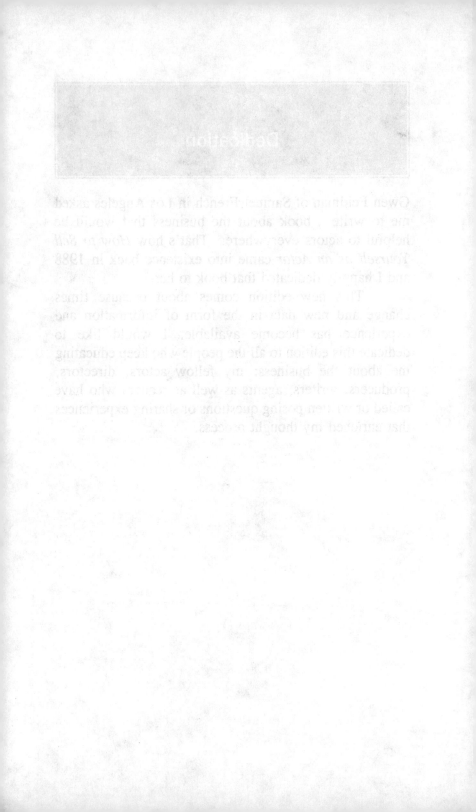

Introduction

Most of us spent our childhood putting on shows for our families, for the neighborhood and/or being in school plays. Many people (whether or not they are planning on pursuing an acting career) are pretty sure they already know how to act or at least can conceptualize the process of learning to act. The concept of translating the acting ability into gainful employment, however, is totally beyond their comprehension. *How to Sell Yourself as an Actor* exists to fill that void. I have crammed as much information regarding 'the business' as I could find or have experienced so far.

The book presents a way of thinking about the business that can help you retain your sense of humor, your sanity and *even* make you feel blessed that the spotlight is not shining on you until you have something to show.

Actors who have been in the business for 20 years and have suddenly decided to 'get serious' have read this book and written to thank me for helping them focus. I, myself, re-read this book from time to time and it helps me remember things I continually forget, so this book is not just for beginners.

You'll get the most out of this book if you read it all the way through, get the concept and then go back and read it again as you begin to formulate your plan of attack. Otherwise, if you are like me, you'll read, start doing a little homework, then get busy and never get back to the core of the book.

There's a real possibility that you might decide

you really don't want to be an actor after you read this book. If the facts sober you now, think how much more sobering they would be after ten years of strife.

If you do decide to go on with your pursuit, no matter what, you will be armed with a clear picture of the cost, legitimate information about what 'it's really like' and enough data to enter the business in an organized and intelligent way.

Whatever you decide to do, start doing it now. You are falling out of an age-range even as we speak. Good luck.

K Callan

August 1992

P. S. I gave up and used masculine pronouns for abstract references. My 'he's' and 'him's' mean he/she and him/her.

Contents

Contents

- 1 -
The Product

A smart businessperson who is going to invest a great deal of time, energy, and money into a new business, does a great deal of research. He interviews people in the field, checks the library for related information and conducts a market survey to see if there is a need for his product. He finds out who his potential customers are, checks to see how much money they have to spend, investigates what they are already buying and endeavors to become a specialist in his field. He realizes he will have to produce a product that is superior, unique, and/or impacts the marketplace in some new way.

It would never occur to most actors to conceptualize their efforts in this manner. Many prefer to believe acting is 'art'. Well, sometimes it may be, but mostly, show-business is about making money; art is extra.

Many people think actors lack the ability to be business-like. I don't think so. I believe many actors just never think about it. There was a time in show business, when one could fantasize about some version of 'being discovered'. In the paternalistic days of yore when film studios signed actors to long indentured contracts, young actors of a certain look were chosen, schooled, groomed and developed by featuring them in ever larger parts until the actors graduated into star-ring parts either as the leading man or woman or the character lead. Although the networks have replaced the studios on some level (they do sign actors for long contracts) there is no way an actor is going to catch an executive's eye without doing the groundwork himself. The financial risks and rewards of the business are so large and the competition so fierce, that an actor's attention to all the facets of selling himself is crucial and may well mean the difference between employment and despair.

Trying to contact a producer, an agent or a casting director without attention to their needs is like spitting in the wind. May as well learn to merchandise the stock and find a way to fit it into what the buyers are willing to spend their money on.

In order to maximize awareness of the actor's strengths and minimize weaknesses, he needs clear, concise answers to the following questions:

- Who am I?
- Why do I want to act?
- Where do I want to act?
- What do I have to offer that is unique?
- When will I start?
- How will I go about it?

Who are You?

Are you white? Black? Chicano? Indian? Male? Female? Old? Young? What difference does it make? It makes a lot of difference; and it makes no difference.

It makes no difference if you are determined to be an actor no matter what. However it makes a lot of difference relative to your chances of making a decent living and living a rewarding life and it greatly impacts how you will be treated in the business.

Therefore, your visible personhood, age, race,

sex and beauty, or lack of it, significantly influences how you will be received in any marketplace.

Why Do You Want to Act?

Do you want to play all the great parts? Are you excited by the process of acting or are you motivated by fame and fortune and your idea of an actor's lifestyle? Several successful actors have confessed in the press that they decided to act in college as a way of meeting girls. Believe me, there are easier ways to meet girls. It's true, successful actors get more than their share of adulation from the opposite sex, but basically, that's true of all successful men and women regardless of their profession.

It's romantic to consider winning your Oscar, driving your Rolls Royce, eating at Spago, kissing beautiful co-stars, and signing autographs, but in reality, it's not fulfilling to walk around New York City every day dropping off pictures to people who not only won't open the door to receive them, but have signs posted saying specifically,

Actors, do not ring our bell.

It's debilitating to be thought of as a necessary evil. It's heartbreaking to be 40 years old and not have a decent place to live. Being perennially unemployed damages the soul.

If you see yourself able to be happy and fulfilled in *any* other endeavor, do it. There is not enough money in the world to compensate for the actor's life. It has to be done for love or you will drop out along the way, bitter, and cranky over the many wasted years.

Where Do You Want to Act?

Do you plan to have a career in your own hometown or are you interested in competing in the major marketplaces of New York and Los Angeles? Do you have a game plan for your hometown? Have you mined all the opportunities in your own backyard? If you are going to assault the larger marketplaces, do you know what that entails?

What Makes You So Special?

What is it about you that would make a director choose you over the thousands of others who are your competition? Are you prettier? Wittier? Uglier? Fatter? Thinner? Is your point of view more informed? What do you want to communicate?

If you are interested in acting as a means of getting approval, forget it. For every 'yes' vote, there will be a thousand rejections.

When Should You Start?

Is this a project you are going to start this minute? Are you waiting until you are out of school? Till your kids are grown? Until you save enough money to quit your current job?

If you are going to be an actor, start as soon as that commitment is clear in your mind. This book is designed to help you look realistically at the profession and the kind of energy, creative thought process and follow-through necessary to market yourself successfully.

How Can I Go About It?

Do you have any idea how to go about it? If I told you to sit down now and write seven pages specifically entailing your game plan, could you do it? You will be able to do exactly that after you have finished reading this book. Keep a notebook. Write down the following:

✓ Who?
✓ Where?
✓ Why?
✓ When?
✓ How?

Pretty soon, you'll be ready to write in some answers.

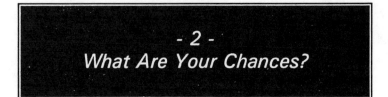

I guess by now all of you have fallen in love at least once and must be aware that love, though delicious, heady, painful and exhilarating, does not necessarily put one in a state of mental clarity for making earth-shaking decisions. You are blind, deaf, euphoric and totally drugged for some period of time before reality sets in and the love object turns out to be just a human being with all the attendant foibles, irritations and faults of the rest of the human race.

One's feelings about being an actor correspond to the above pretty closely. Totally unrealistic, just driven. That being the case, I would like to put things into some type of perspective. This is not to break up the relationship, but actually to further it.

It's time to evaluate whether *you* and an *acting* profession are right for each other. Let's look at the basics (forgetting about specialness and talent until later) and find out whether your sex, age, ethnic, physical and emotional package suit your choice of career.

Whether you like it or not, it is true, your face is your fortune or to be more pragmatic:

Physicality Is Destiny

Author Nikki Finke's feature on Kathy Bates entitled "Great Isn't Good Enough" in the Calendar section of the Los Angeles Times, January 27, 1991, tells the story very accurately:

• *'You're really not attractive enough for daytime TV,'*
Bates was told by a soap opera casting director. John
Simon wrote in a review of Bates' performance in the
Off-Broadway production of "Frankie and Johnnie in
the Clair de Lune" that it was 'unfortunate' her
leading man 'should play opposite an actress who,
even for a midnight snacker, is enormously
overweight.'

In the same article, Bates is quoted:

• *I found out when I came out to Hollywood that it*
was all looks-oriented. And it was frustrating. At
times, it was something that was really vicious I've
had to deal with.

It's true in any walk of life: People who are beautiful
have it easier. I, too, like to gaze at beautiful people.
I find that beauty nourishes me, whether it is a beautiful day, a walk at the ocean or smelling a lovely
flower. This is not to say you *have* to be beautiful, I
believe you can look like Quasimodo and have a career
if you really believe in yourself and pursue your
dream in a focused way.

We could debate the relative merits of being
beautiful and thus being deprived of the struggle to
prove oneself. The reality that the beautiful one will
probably never be developed to his/her full potential
on other levels doesn't matter. *Beauty* wins.

So Do Men

Since films, plays, and television reflect the world
surrounding us, it's no surprise that there is more
opportunity for any man to work than any woman.

As a member of the Academy of Motion Picture Arts and Sciences, I am privileged to attend screenings of the films eligible for consideration for the Academy Awards. Every year, a majority of the films feature 25 to 30 men in a cast with possibly two women, frequently both of whom were blonde, beautiful, 18 and naked. Meryl Streep, keynote speaker at the Screen Actors Guild's first annual women's conference in 1990, summed up the dilemma for women:

• *We all know what the problem is. There's very little work for women. And when we do work, we get paid much less than our male counterparts.*

Who Makes The Money?

Screen Actors Guild conducted a statistical survey of the status of women in film, television and commercials in August of 1991.

• *Females earned less than half as much as their male counterparts last year under Screen Actors Guild contracts, but are slowly - very slowly closing the gap, according to the latest figures compiled by SAG.*
In 1989, males earned a whopping $348 million more than did their female counterparts. That gap was narrowed to $343 million last year.
Last year, SAG males earned nearly $668 million under all SAG contracts (including residuals) - or more than twice the $325 million earned by SAG females.
In 1989, however, the earnings gap was even larger. In 1989, males earned $644 million, while white females earned $296 million.
Part of the disparity is due to the fact that far

*more males are employed in films and tv shows than
are females. Another part of the disparity is due to the
fact that women, when they are employed on films and
tv shows, only earn, on average, approximately 74%
of what their male colleagues earn. That disparity,
however, also has been closing. Five years ago the
average working actress earned only 70% of what her
average male colleague earned.*

*The gap in job opportunities is most prominent
in supporting roles. Last year males were cast in
21,546 supporting roles, while women were cast in
only 10,568.*

"Femme Earnings Sag at SAG" -
Kathleen O'Steen
Daily Variety
August 15, 1991

In an earlier Screen Actors Guild survey, earnings
were broken down into age groups:

• *After the age of 10, men earn consistently higher
average annual earnings under SAG contracts than
women do. The discrepancy increases with age as
women's average earnings drop significantly in the
40's, 50's and 60's while men's earnings peak in these
age groups. Many more females (one-third) than
males (one-quarter) had no SAG earnings at all in
1989.*

*Feature films are heavily dominated by men,
with nearly 71% of all 9,440 roles in 1989 going to
men - - more than twice the number given to women.
Television programming is only somewhat better, with
35.4% of all 39,161 roles going to women and 64.6%*

going to men.

The Female in Focus: In Whose Image?
"A Statistical Survey
of the Status of Women in Film
Television & Commercials"
Screen Actors Guild
August 1, 1990

The Philadelphia Inquirer Sunday magazine details the situation even more depressingly in an article entitled "Too Male and Too Pale":

• *According to Screen Actors Guild, actresses make 50 cents for every dollar earned by their male counter-parts. This is significantly lower than the national average for working women. The Bureau of Labor Statistics reports that American females earn seventy-one cents on the 'male dollar.'*

"Too Male & Too Pale" -
Carrie Rickey
The Philadelphia Inquirer
March 24, 1991

America is not alone in trivializing its actresses:

• *London - It was not exactly a surprise to those working in the British entertainment industry, but now it's been documented for the first time: Actresses in Britain are paid about half of what their male counterparts earn.*

"British Study:
Actresses Paid Less Than Actors" -
Jeff Kaye
The Los Angeles Times
March 6, 1992

The same article went on to relate that British management puts its actresses 'out to pasture' even sooner than American producers:

• *The Equity report also revealed a significant disparity between the ages that men and women work most frequently in Britain. Women have more opportunities for work while they are younger than 30, whereas the busiest period for men continues into their 40s. Women also play younger parts than their actual age in comparison to men.*

On the other hand, Cher is philosophical about it:

• *I'm not into that thing about women and films. It's hard for women anywhere. Hollywood is no different. I get paid more money than I could possibly imagine. I'm a woman and I make tons of money. I don't make as much as a man, but that's just the way it's set up. That's the reality of the way we live, but we still get paid an unbelievable amount of money to do what we would all do for nothing.*
>   "The Cher Conundrum" -
>   Hilary De Vries
>   The Los Angeles Times
>   November 3, 1991

Leading men make the money. That usually means *white* leading men. Leading women make money, but not as much and not for as long. If you are entrepreneurs like Jane Fonda or Barbra Streisand, you can actually become powerful and have a career that spans generations, but that is rare. Sad to say, women's lib notwithstanding, women still are considered ornamental or less. They are condescended to rather than respected.

Character men and women can make good money in television, but Randy Quaid will never make as much money as Dennis Quaid.

In 1983, the Screen Actors Guild Affirmative Action Committee conducted a survey that showed:

• *Only about 30% of SAG members earn their total income in performance media. 65% report working only one or two SAG jobs per year, with five or fewer days on the set.*

70% supplement their performance income in a wide range of jobs and other sources, many in such creative arenas as writing, photography and teaching. Many members own their own businesses. Women tend to work in modeling, retail establishments, restaurants and offices; while men are more inclined to work as skilled laborers or office workers. Older performers often work as acting teachers.

New Yorkers find most of their supplemental income in the legitimate theater, bars and restaurants; while West Coast performers earn more in office positions and film support services.

Generally, young white men work more and earn more than women, minorities and those over 40.
Screen Actor
Fall 1987

Although these figures are from a few years ago, 1990 Screen Actors Guild numbers imply that matters have gotten even worse:

Screen Actors Guild 1990 Earning Survey

• *29% earned no money at all.*

59% earned from $1 to $20,000.
5.9% earned from $20,001 to $50,000.
2.6% earned from $50,001 to $100,000.
2.8% earned $100,000 or more.

If you do the math, you'll see that only 11.3% members of SAG earned over $20,000 in 1990. <u>Daily Variety</u>'s article about those statistics expanded on the bad news:

• *SAG members have been hard-hit by the recession. The latest earnings report found that nearly two-thirds of all Screen Actors Guild members earned less in 1991 than they did in 1990, and that total SAG income dropped by 2.2% last year - the biggest year-to-year earnings decline in more than 20 years. The report also found that the average income of SAG members dropped by 5.3% - from $12,596 in 1990 to an estimated $11,920 last year.*

> "Actors' '91 Income Drop
> Called Worst in 20 Years" -
> David Robb
> Hollywood Reporter
> March 24, 1992

Minorities

These statistics do not take into consideration the even smaller number of jobs available to actors who are not perceived as people who could have come from Nebraska or Iowa. Being ethnic (visibly Jewish, Italian, Hispanic, Asian, etc.) cuts down on your employment opportunities even more.

It's only in the recent past that 'black is beautiful' as far as making a living in show business.

There are an increasing number of films with predominantly black casts. Morgan Freeman is now hot. Danny Glover, Wesley Snipes and Denzel Washington are big stars and television shows such as "A Different World" and "In Living Color" are produced by, directed by and star people of color. Even commercials reflect the fact that America is no longer able to ignore it's growing population of people of color. Arsenio Hall and Oprah Winfrey have proved that black performers can appeal to Iowa as much as David Letterman and Phil Donahue.

Black directors and writers are also breaking through in film as evidenced by Spike Lee, Robert Townsend and the brilliant John Singleton, who was nominated for an Academy Award for directing his first film, "Boyz in the Hood." No one handed these men their 'break' and all of these men not only directed, but wrote their films. In most cases, they raised the money for their projects as well. Did you know that Robert Townsend, who directed "Hollywood Shuffle," financed it with credit card advances?

Because the public is unaccustomed to seeing people of color *at all*, this work appears to be *great* progress. And it is. But it still represents a very small percentage of the overall pie.

Lest anyone jump to the conclusion that higher black employment has anything to do with affirmative action, talent or fairness, let's be clear. More blacks are working because this reflects the growing economic clout of the black community.

You Think You've Got It Bad

Black women have an even tougher time than black men or white women:

● *'While the situation right now for women is not OK, for black women it's hopeless,' says Screen Actors Guild affirmative-action administrator, Rodney Mitchell. 'I can point out any number of ingenues poised for stardom - - Demi Moore, Winona Ryder, but I defy you to name any women of color poised for prominence.'*

> "Too Male and Too Pale" -
> Carrie Rickey
> The Philadelphia Inquirer
> March 26, 1991

And for other Ethnic women, the situation is even worse:

● *Ethnic women have remarkably few opportunities in film and television today. Of the 34% of all film and TV roles that go to women, blacks get 9.5%, Latino/ Hispanics get 3.1%, Asian-Pacifics get 2.6% and American Indians are nearly off the chart with only 0.1% of all female roles.*

> "The Female in Focus, In Whose
> Image: A Statistical Survey of
> the State of Women in
> Film, Television & Commercials" -
> Screen Actor
> August 1, 1990

In the September 24, 1991 issue of Daily Variety, David Robb writes:

● *In a 30-page report on the status of blacks in the entertainment industry, the National Association for the Advancement of Colored People charged that blacks are 'under-represented in every aspect of the television and film industry' and that top decision-making positions are 'totally dominated by white males.'*

The report, titled 'Out Of Focus - Out Of Sync,' found that black actresses 'are becoming increasingly invisible on the movie screen,' and that 'nepotism,' 'cronyism' and 'racial discrimination' have resulted in a 'paucity of black executives' at networks and studios.

"NAACP Cites Nepotism, Cronyism, Bias" -
David Robb
Daily Variety
September 24, 1991

Research Your Employment Opportunities

Explore the subject: Spend every night for a month in front of the television set with a paper and pencil. Assuming you were trained and in the right place at the right time, are there parts for you? On commercials? On night time television? On daytime television? This exercise works whether or not you intend to go the major marketplace.

Assess carefully who you are physically and the impact this has on your earning power. Men who are extremely tall and have any natural grace and athletic ability are recruited to be basketball players. If you are a gifted athlete who yearns to be a basketball star, but are only five feet tall, all the heart and determination in the world isn't going to make you into Larry Bird.

This applies to actors as well. Look at your natural talents. Will you physically fit into a casting niche in the business? Consider yourself in relation to the people who are working: are you the right age? Do you need to be older to logically sell who you are?

If you do, you don't have to starve while you age, there are alternatives. I was conducting a New York seminar for the American Film Institute when a very off-beat, not traditionally attractive, 30ish man came up and spoke to me. He had a job in local television in Connecticut and had been considering making the move to the big marketplace in New York City. Until the seminar, he had not really analyzed the fact that he is a character man who has not yet grown into himself and that he will be more physically employable in 15 years. Since he's already employed in the business, he decided to continue growing into himself where he is and post-pone the move to New York until his visual age catches up to his presence.

I remember seeing Geraldine Page in an interview when she was nominated for an Academy Award for "The Pope of Greenwich Village." She had spent the previous several years totally unemployable. She said:

• *I don't know who it is that has finally decided it's okay for me to work again.*

In fact, she had just been through a growth period where she was changing from one type to another, *visually*.

Cinematic Age

I recently spoke to a friend of mine who is a very successful actress who was preparing for a new film and was in the midst of make-up tests. My friend is 59 years old and looks great. In the film, she plays a 62-year-old woman.

In trying to make her look 62, the make-up

men applied a latex film to her face. She told them it was ridiculous. In three years, she would *be* 62. She won't look *that* different. All the people she knows that are 62 look at least 10 years younger than the 'age' the make-up men created.

The make-up department explained that, *cinematically*, people expect a 62-year-old person to appear a particular way. If you are a 62-year-old person who announces you have a 35-year-old son and a 15-year-old granddaughter and people say, *You look so young, we'd never know it*, the movie-going public isn't going to buy it, either.

What They See Is What They Get

When I first went to New York, I made a lot of money in commercials. There were several reasons why I was successful, not the least of which was my 'midwestern American face,' a gift from my parents for which I can take no credit.

As successful as I was in New York in commercials, when I moved to Los Angeles that particular success did not translate. In Los Angeles, they prefer prettier people. I was perfect as a 'real' person in New York. In Los Angeles, reality is not the strong suit.

Because I was on the crest of an age category change, I did fewer commercials in Los Angeles. No longer the mother of young kids, I was moving into 'mother of the bride' territory. Not only are there not *that* many parts for 'MOB's,' there were others more securely in that age range, who were cinematically better able to fill that role. Interestingly, this 'image' problem did not interfere with my film and television career during that period. Go figure.

Actors pass through many age ranges during their careers. Some will be lucrative. Others dismal. Because of age and overexposure, everything can stop with no warning. One day you are doing great, finally heaving a sigh of relief,

Oh, boy, it's going to work out. I'm not going to have to worry for a while.

And then it's over for 6 months, or a year, or a year-and-a-half. I don't know a single actor who has been in the business for any length of time who has not had this experience. I've been told that 'no young, excited actor is going to believe this will ever happen to him' and I do agree that I wouldn't have believed it either. But no one *ever* told me about age ranges and changes and when I experienced this phenomena for the first time, it was pretty disillusioning. You think, it's all over, that you'll never work again, and that you are the only person in the world to have this experience. It would have helped a bit if I had been able to say,

'I never believed it would happen, but at least, I know it's part of the process and not just me. Now, I believe.'

Jimmy Cota, one of the partners of the prestigious Artists Agency in Los Angeles, put it this way:

• *Look at the business. A growing number of shows; the magazine shows, the reality shows, and game shows don't use actors. Sit-coms use only one or two guest stars. The amount of money available to the community is somewhat diminished. What you have is a number of people who were able to make a living who can no longer make a living. The movies are all youth-market movies with 16-17 year old kids. Once they're 23 and can no longer play seniors in high school anymore, the business slows down for them.*

The Spring, 1992 edition of Screen Actor agrees:

• *No-actor factor. Cheaper news and reality shows that hire few actors are rapidly replacing dramatic programs. Animation is also booming, employing voice artists, but no on-camera stars who might demand perks or profits.*
"Bad News" -
Compiled by Mark Locher
Screen Actor
Spring 1992, Vol. 31, No. 1

• *We know in the television area that there's been a substantial change in network schedules, shifting from the one-hour dramatic shows to reality-based shows, which means less employment for a lot of people.*
What people may be able to anticipate are smaller productions and maybe fewer shooting days.
"Prod'n Pace Picks Up" -
Kathleen O'Steen
Daily Variety
April 1, 1992

• *Increasingly, the networks are choosing cut-rate, quasi-news shows such as "Rescue 911" on CBS or ABC's "FBI, The Untold Stories" over costly dramas. Once dominant in prime time, drams account now for*

only about 30% of the program schedule.
"Too Costly for Prime Time" -
John Lippman
The Los Angeles Times
March 22, 1992

Emotional Strength

Do you have the temperament to withstand the stress of constant unemployment and daily rejection? New York agent, Jerry Hogan told me he began his career as an actor, but stopped when he realized his nature couldn't handle constant rejection. The wear and tear on his ego was too much.

Of course, I contend that actors do not really go into acting because they are necessarily in their right minds. My theory is we are all drawn to this business because we come from a background of real or imagined rejection. We are, therefore, familiar with the feeling and have ways of coping with it. If we are lucky, we get healthier along the way. Sometimes we stay in the business because we are making more money than we could make anyplace else. And sometimes we leave.

It's time to get out your notebook again and add:

✓ physicality is destiny
✓ white men make the money
✓ women work considerably less after age 40
✓ check the marketplace for appropriate jobs
✓ real age/cinematic age
✓ emotional strength

Many people have neither the drive, interest nor emotional skills to be businesslike, focused, relentless and positive in the face of adversity. If you do have these traits, it's important to consider now which marketplace will answer your needs.

In this business, geography can significantly affect your destiny. Shelley Duvall was a local Houston actress when director Robert Altman came to town and cast her in "Brewster McCloud." Once she had film credits, she moved to Hollywood and starred in "McCabe and Mrs. Miller," "Nashville," "The Shining," "Popeye" and other films. Today she is also the innovative producer of "Faerie Tale Theatre" and produces for cable via her own production company: Think Entertainment.

If she had been in Los Angeles during the time Altman was casting the film, it's possible she might never have gotten the attention of the casting director since the talent pool in Los Angeles is so vast that it's easy to get lost in the shuffle. In Los Angeles, the competition is not only all the other actors in the country who have come to 'the big orange,' but the New York actor (quite different in character and training than a Los Angeles actor) and all the old movie stars, television stars and people who have recognizable faces from short-lived television series. They are not necessarily better-trained or more talented than you, but they are more visible and that's the name of the game. More and more films and network television shows are leaving NY/LA and filming in smaller venues. This could be important to you. In the late '50s, there was a television show called "Route 66" that shot all around the country. When they came to my home town to shoot, as a member of the local talent pool, I was immediately called in to audition and more than elated to get (as my parents termed it) 'a real acting job with Hollywood people'. I'm sure I'm not the only one who got to qualify for my Screen Actors Guild card in my own hometown on network television as a result of that show.

Although at that point in my life I thought I was going to spend the rest of my life primarily as a homemaker, that experience certainly gave me the feeling that I had something to sell in the larger marketplace. The validation made it easier to have the courage to make the big move to New York when my life changed.

Where the Work Is

Screen Actors Guild's quarterly magazine, "Screen Actor" regularly presents a wealth of information regarding the business and where it is heading. The information they provide is sometimes quite surprising. Did you know, for instance, that Washington, D. C. is the fastest growing SAG branch in the country?

• *Conventional wisdom holds that New York and Los Angeles are the 'best' places for performers to build and maintain their careers. Indeed, these two production centers accounted for more than 90% of SAG's record one billion dollars in total earnings in 1990. But New York and Los Angeles are clearly not the only places where work is available. Chicago, San Francisco, Florida, Washington, D. C. and Detroit offer many performers the opportunity to live and work away from the harried, competitive environments of the major markets. Even the smaller cities have become sophisticated in luring location shoots in their areas.*

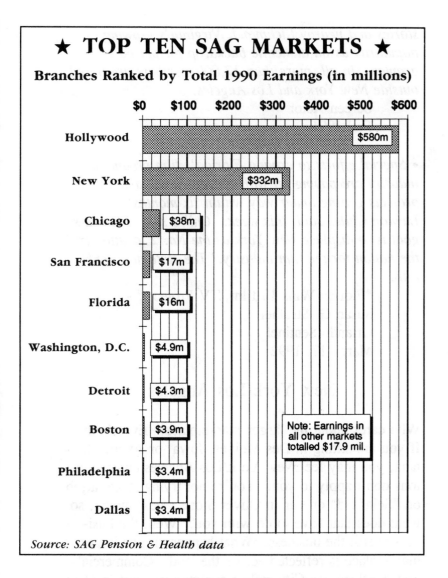

★ TOP TEN SAG MARKETS ★

Branches Ranked by Total 1990 Earnings (in millions)

Hollywood	$580m
New York	$332m
Chicago	$38m
San Francisco	$17m
Florida	$16m
Washington, D.C.	$4.9m
Detroit	$4.3m
Boston	$3.9m
Philadelphia	$3.4m
Dallas	$3.4m

Note: Earnings in all other markets totalled $17.9 mil.

Source: SAG Pension & Health data

*Reprinted with permission from Screen Actors Guild
Screen Actor
Fall 1991*

Part of Washington D. C.'s recent success, for example, is attributable to more government themed

*stories and nearby Richmond, Virginia's growing
popularity as an authentic backdrop for period
dramas. In all, more than 17,000 members are based
outside New York and Los Angeles.*
>Screen Actor
>Fall 1991

• *'Special efforts to expand Florida's film production
industry are paying off with 13 new movie and TV
projects getting under way within six months'. Gov.
Lawton Chiles said, this week. Chiles said 'Florida's
goal is to displace New York as the No. 2 location in
the nation for the film industry.' The state now ranks
third.*
>"Florida Wins 13 film, TV Projects" -
>Susan G. Strother
>Orlando Sentinel
>March 17, 1992

New York/Los Angeles

Who cares about the larger marketplace? Everybody!
If you are sitting in Des Moines, Iowa or Avon, Mon-
tana, you may feel New York/Los Angeles considerations don't apply to you. You're not trying to get a job
on "Seinfield" or star in Oliver Stone's next movie, so
what does that have to do with you? Well, the business is still the business. What happens in the larger
marketplace is reflected across the land. Commercials
cast in Oklahoma City reflect commercials cast in New
York City. New York commercials always follow
trends set by current films and also set trends for the
rest of the nation.

Plays performed in Dayton, Ohio were on
Broadway or in Los Angeles a few years ago. We are

all one. If you are going to market a product, it is important to have data on various aspects of merchandising. This includes learning how to produce a superlative product. You don't have to make a practical decision (if you were practical, you probably would not be an actor), but at least you should have the facts before you.

Preparing The Product

If you are reading this book as a student preparing to study, I urge you consider one of the important theatre schools if you can afford it and if they accept you. It does make a difference where you are educated. Not only are some schools significantly superior to others, but there is a group of schools that is universally accepted as the most comprehensive training for young actors and whose cachet instantly alerts the antennae of employers.

At one time, these schools were referred to as "The Leagues" and were banded together as Schools of Professional Training for Actors which offered proscribed rigorous conservatory training.

Although that official collective no longer exists, those schools still offer graduates who are immediately thought by buyers (casting directors, agents, producers, directors, etc.) to be the *creme de la creme* of new young actors, surely where the next Meryl Streep and Paul Newman are coming from (and did).

If you graduate from one of the prestigious theatre schools, you are definitely ahead of the game as far as agents in NY/LA are concerned. And in fact, you probably *will* be better trained. Actors in these programs are routinely scouted by agents and sometimes procure representation as early as their freshman year.

Prestigious Theatre Schools

* **American Conservatory Theatre**
Edward Hastings
450 Geary Street
San Francisco, CA 94102
(415) 749-2200

American Repertory Theatre
Robert Brustein, Artistic Director
Harvard University
Byerly Hall, 8 Garden Street
Cambridge, Massachusetts 02138
(617) 495-2668

* **Boston University**
Robert Morgan
121 Bay State Road
Boston, Massachusetts 02215
(617) 353-2300

* **Carnegie Mellon**
Elisabeth Orion
5000 Forbes Avenue
Pittsburgh, Pennsylvania 15213
(412) 268-2082

Catholic University
William H. Graham, Chairperson
620 Michigan Ave. NE
Washington, District of Columbia 20064
(202) 319-5358

* **Juilliard School**
Michael Langham
Lincoln Center
New York City, New York 10023
(212) 799-5000

* **New York University**
Arthur Barstow, Chairperson
25 West 4th Street
New York City, New York 10012
(212) 998-1212

* **North Carolina School of the Arts**
Robert Francesconi
200 Waughtown Street
Winston-Salem, North Carolina 27717-2189
(919) 770-3399

* **Southern Methodist University**
Dean Charlie Helfert
P. O. Box 286
Dallas, Texas 75275
(214) 692-3217

* **State University of New York (at Purchase)**
Israel Hicks
735 Anderson Hill Road
Purchase, New York 10577
(914) 251-6000

* **University of California (at San Diego)**
Adele Shank, Chairperson
101 Administration Bldg. 2nd floor
La Jolla, California 92093
(619) 534-6889

Yale Drama School
Yale University
Dean Lloyd Richards
P. O. Box 1302 A
Yale Station
New Haven, Connecticut 06520
(203) 432-1505

*   formerly in the Leagues collective.

All of these schools offer excellent training, but they are hard to get into and very expensive, so be wise and investigate more than one. This type of education requires a big commitment of time and money. Consider carefully in order to choose the school that is right for you.

Options

If you want to be an actor because you want to play Macbeth or Lady Macbeth, perhaps you can do that in your own hometown. You can join the local theatre group and have a rewarding time. You might play bigger parts with more regularity than you ever would as a professional actor. If you are really serious about acting all the great parts, perhaps you will become a repertory actor. There are interesting rep groups all over the country.

In Costa Mesa, a seaside community southeast of Los Angeles, there is a core group of actors who have worked together since producers Martin Benson and David Emmes created South Coast Repertory (SCR) over 20 years ago. These actors have played hundreds of parts. They don't make huge salaries, but they make a decent wage, are highly thought of within their community and they make their living doing what they love. They certainly embody the term 'working actor'. SCR received a Tony in 1988 in recognition of their contribution to theatre in general, and to play-wrights in particular.

Actors Equity Association will send you (@ .25 each) lists of theaters across the country which include the specific categories of dinner theatre, Broadway, small theatre, etc. You might want to call them first and find out what's available. There are six lists in all. For $1.50 plus a self-addressed-stamped envelope, you can get all of them.

Actors Equity	Actors Equity
6430 Sunset Blvd.	165 W. 46th St.
Hollywood, CA 90028	New York, NY 10036
213-462-2334	212-869-8530

Entertainment Auditioning Centers

There are several theater conferences around the country that hold annual auditions for actors.

Straw Hat, Box 1187 in **Port Chester, New York 10573** provides a place for non-Equity actors to audition for multiple theaters on the East Coast (30 theaters) and on the West Coast (15 theaters) in February and March. It costs $30 to participate in one or $40 for both. You can get on the list in the Fall. When you write, be sure to include a stamped, self-addressed #10 envelope. You don't have to send money until you are accepted.

The New England Theatre Conference (NETC), c/o Dept. Theatre, North Eastern University, Boston, Massachusetts 02115. is another terrific resource. 56 Equity and non-Equity theaters attend their March auditions. They routinely receive 1200-1500 applications and choose 500. The cost to be a member of NETC is $25. I don't think this includes a fee for participating in a particular audition, but either way it seems to be worth the money. This organization provides so much information and opportunity for employment that I couldn't write it all down over the phone. My advice is to become a member and get their newsletter. NETC has opportunities and information for actors *and* technicians on every level.

Other programs that screen talent for pro-fessional theaters are **East Coast Theatre Conference** at **Montclair State College** in **Montclair, New Jersey** and **The Southeastern Theatre Conference (SETC)** in **Greensboro, North Carolina.**

Staying Home

There may be many opportunities for work in your own community that have not occurred to you. If you intend to enter the national marketplace, the best thing you can do is spend a number of years in your own city exploiting and developing all of your talents.

When I was working at the Cherry County Playhouse in Traverse City, Michigan a few years ago, our cast frequented a restaurant that had three shows nightly featuring singing, dancing and skits. This work was gruelling, demanding and didn't pay a lot, but the young entertainers who were fortunate enough to get these summer jobs, were, in essence, being paid to go to graduate school. These students all found their jobs though notices at their local colleges.

Worthy, Livable Goals

Acting is a *very small piece of the pie.* You will have a much greater chance of success if you can say up front:

I want to learn everything I can about show business on every level and then make a decision about where I can be the happiest and most productive.

Not only will you be able to make a more informed decision about your life's work, but you will be much happier on the road to your destination.

It's always hard to break into a closed system, whether it is show business or IBM, but if you allow yourself to go through any door that is open, instead of waiting for 'the one', your chances are greatly enhanced. Not only are you likely to find work sooner, but you may find a better niche that would have never occurred to you.

Hard as it might be to believe, acting is looked upon as the lowest rung of the creative ladder by the rest of the creative community.

When I lived in Dallas as a young woman, it was a whole lot easier to make money as a director than as an actor, so I directed. I also wrote and produced. Not at any high level, you understand, but, I did whatever was available. If I had come to New York or Los Angeles then, I would have done all those things there. At that point my mind was totally open; I was pretty clear about the fact that I didn't know a lot, so I asked anyone I could corner for advice and help. I just wanted to be engaged in theatre, film or television.

It didn't occur to me to want to play Lady

Macbeth, all I really knew was that show business looked like a way to escape my life. Anything that smacked of show business looked like a movie to me and I wanted to do it. It's great when you are young and just starting; you have no image to protect.

The first day of acting class in college, I remember Mrs. Hardy telling us that we should take *any* opportunity to get up in front of people. What a gift she gave me. Until that time, I had thought people would think I was 'pushy' or 'stuck on myself' or 'conceited', but now I had been told, that as part of my training, I should take every chance. I can still remember the sense of freedom I felt.

Who knows? People probably did think I was stupid, pushy, crazy or worse. It didn't matter for I was on a mission. From where I am sitting now, I can only wish that my aspirations had been higher. Although I was willing to do whatever it took, my mind was clearly set on acting. Today, I realize that actors with truly great careers did not just act.

• *For all her well-known setbacks in the 1930's, from her disastrous 1933 Broadway appearance in "The Lake" (which inspired Dorothy Parker's famous putdown that she ran 'the gamut of emotions from A to B') Katherine Hepburn never had trouble making her own opportunities. She had the wherewithal to tie up the film rights to "The Philadelphia Story," the Broadway vehicle that she knew she could ride to a Hollywood comeback.*
"A Wild Desire to Be Absolutely Fascinating" - Frank Rich
The New York Times Book Review
September 29, 1991

So open your brain. Let your goal be to be successful in showbusiness - wherever that takes you. Some of the best directors I have ever worked with were once actors and they would never trade in the power and vision they command as directors for the mere visibility of being an actor. Many writers and producers from acting backgrounds feel the same way.

What Can I Do At Home?

There are many advantages to staying home:

o   You get to stay with the people you love.
o   You live in a familiar environment.
o   It's cheaper anyplace than NY/LA (except San Francisco).
o   You already have a support group.

Just because you are going to stay home (wherever that is) doesn't mean you can't keep abreast of what is happening in the large entertainment centers. When I was pursuing my career in Texas which included directing and producing, I made it a point to see every New York touring production that came to town and was able to pick up all kinds of lighting and staging ideas I would never have thought of on my own.

Besides staying up-to-date on the business, it's important to assess what jobs are available and how you can fit into the existing scheme of things.

When I was in high school trying to figure out how one goes from studying acting and being in local plays to making the jump into the big time, I decided to write my MGM musical idols for advice. Among the three people I wrote (who *all* answered me) were The late Gower Champion and his wife, Marge. Star dancers for MGM then, Gower later became an important director and choreographer on Broadway and Marge also now directs. Marge wrote me a wonderfully warm and detailed letter telling me that the best thing to do was to stay in Dallas until I had done everything there was to do in my hometown and *then* go to New York and study at The Neighborhood Playhouse or with Herbert Berghof at The HB Studios. I followed her advice, and even though I didn't get to New York until 15 years later, she was still right.

Unless you are drop-dead beautiful and your beauty is going to die on the vine, there is every reason for you to refine your craft in a more protected environment. Then you can enter the bigger marketplace with training, credits and hopefully, a savings account.

Although you may not be able to make a living as an actor on the stage in your home town (that's pretty hard to do even in Los Angeles and New York), there are many variations on that theme that offer a chance to make money.

Stand-Up Comedy

Put together a stand-up act. If there are no comedy clubs in your area (which seems unlikely), call local service organizations like The Lions Club and The Jaycees. They are always looking for entertaining speakers for their functions. Charge at least $50, and remember, the more they pay you, the more they respect you.

Putting together an act is not as formidable as it seems. Just do it one joke at a time. A way to build material that is perfect for you is to sit down and make a list of things that make you angry: the guy who parks in the handicapped zone while you are a good person who obeys the rules, people who cut in front of you on the freeway, others who won't let you 'in' the freeway lane, those who speed up 'just enough' to beat you to the checkout line at the grocery store, etc. There's a universality of humor in all our pet peeves. Tap into that. Just try to get one minute together, then five. Try the jokes out on your friends (but don't tell them you're auditioning your material) then volunteer to be master of ceremonies at some function and try out your material. When you have 20 minutes - call those clubs and get hired.

Perhaps you could be the weather forecaster on your local television station. Weathermen/women in the major markets are frequently cast from the ranks of stand-up comedians. As a matter of fact, stand-up comedians are considered such ripe potentials for television situation comedies, casting directors from Los Angeles regularly monitor comedy club operations all over the country.

Book Reviews

Most people think of book reviews as being something you *read*, in fact there are actors who make a nice living by reading a current best seller, compiling a sort of 'verbal Cliff's Notes' and presenting it for various service organizations as entertainment. I always wanted to do a book review with a stack of 8x10s of famous actors and casting the parts as I tell the story; *This part should be played by Elizabeth Taylor* (and hold up her picture) and so on. They will immediately know just what you are talking about. Have a 10, a 15, and a 20 minute version prepared and tailor the material to the needs of the audience.

Local Radio & Television

Call your local stations and ask what the possibilities are for employment on the air. If there is no one to talk to there, look in the Yellow Pages under advertising agencies and call them. Ask who hires on camera or radio talent, note the name and ask to speak to him. Say something like:

Hi, I'm Mary Smith. I'm an actress and I'm interested in finding out who hires actors for commercials.

When you get that person on the phone, reintroduce yourself and say that you would like to come by and meet him. If you have a picture and resume, mention that. If you have done any jobs that might impress, mention those.

When you call, do so late in the day. Frequently the secretary is gone and your future employer will pick up his own phone. Be up, personable, brief, energetic and specific. Arrange a meeting. Go. Be on time. Be professional and be strong. Don't play 'like-me-like-me' but do indicate that you are willing to learn and are a hard worker. Show that by arriving early. Make sure you have read the morning newspaper so that you can have something interesting to talk about other than yourself.

If that person can't help you, ask him for advice on who else to speak to or what to do next. People love to give advice.

Cable

In every marketplace, there are locally produced cable television shows. You can actually produce your own.

You don't even need a camera. In Los Angeles, there is a bargain shopper on a major local news show whose career started when she produced her own weekly cable access show. Today, she also writes a weekly news column in "The Los Angeles Times." A young comic I know produced a funny restaurant guide show that is now part of CBS nightly local Los Angeles news.

Teach or Start Your Own Theatre

It's not that difficult to get a job teaching acting at a local school or at the YMCA/YWCA. Decide whether you want to teach children, teenagers or adults or all of the above. You can put notices up in your local supermarket, church, or post office announcing your classes.

Teaching is not only a means of making money and feeling fulfilled, but it also focuses one's thinking and makes one a better actor. Degreed credentials are helpful, though by no means essential. We all have encountered teachers without heart, empathy, insight and passion who had very impressive degrees, but were not inspiring in any way. Great teachers (and great directors) arouse the actor's passion and motivate him to resonate in ways he never thought of. If you feel you don't know how to teach, pattern your work on the best acting teacher you ever had and read books by great teachers (Allan Miller's book, "A Passion for Acting" or Uta Hagen's book "Respect for Acting") for inspiration. I also really love Michael Shurtleff's book "Audition" for acting insight whether as an actor or as a teacher.

Whatever your format, find a way to present your students before the public. Write or find plays that have to do with the holiday of the moment and produce something short. It's no fun to study acting and then having no place to show it off.

Or start your own theatre and teach acting on the side. That way your students can have the possibility of auditioning for your productions. Choose a play you love that has a small cast and one set. It's not that hard.

More things to write in your notebook:

✓ opportunities at home
✓ the big marketplaces
✓ study
✓ all the options
✓ worthy livable goals
✓ hometown advantage and options

Now that you know about the opportunities that exist at home, you are ready to explore the most important questions of all.

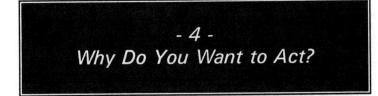

Life is very short. I tell my kids this all the time. Youth is over in about 15 minutes. Therefore it is important not to squander what our society prizes as the most energetic, attractive part of life by chasing a rainbow whose pot of gold may not be what you want.

Just because acting seems to appeal to others doesn't mean it would appeal to you. I sometimes think the unavailability of the jobs is the thing that appeals to actors the most. Maybe if everybody chose me I wouldn't even be interested. So far, that hasn't been a problem.

What is it about acting that appeals to you? Are you truly interested in the process of creating a character? Does being a psychological sleuth attract you? Do you have some need to communicate? Are you an exhibitionist? Are your feelings about acting based on any realistic appraisal of what an actor's life is all about?

I was raised on a diet of movie musicals, and as a five-year old could easily tell that Betty Grable and Esther Williams seemed to be living a much more exciting life than any grownups I ever saw. In Dallas, no handsome men were bringing bouquets of long-stemmed red roses to anybody. I had the idea being an actress was something like "The Dolly Sisters," or any one of a number of those old 20th Century Fox movies depicting life backstage.

After twenty years in the business, I must tell

you, that for me at least, life as an actress has not been like a Betty Grable musical. Men *have* brought me long-stemmed red roses, but it had little to do with my being an actress. Well, maybe a little.

But the point is, I never saw Betty or Esther running around town picking up scripts, having to create an appropriate emotional climate for themselves to work in, auditioning for a room full of executives who had already seen ten other actresses who looked just like them. I never saw them rush from one appointment to another, changing hairdos and clothes at red lights, dealing with parking and surly secretaries while trying to stay centered and concentrated on audition material. I'm not knocking this. I'm tickled to have an audition to go to. I just didn't have the faintest notion that acting involved these things.

I never saw Betty or Esther take an acting class or work with the flu or worry about a sick child. But then, they never had children in those stories either. Just roses. They never passed through age categories that put them out of work for years. It seemed they changed from young and adorable to middle-aged and responsible and then grandparent material in a cinematically authentic manner, without a hitch.

Of course, in real life, neither of those ladies had a life long career. Betty phased out when she got a little older and Marilyn came in. And Esther quit the business when she married Fernando Lamas.

Before You Study Acting
Study the Life-Style

In order to make an intelligent decision about acting as a way to spend your life, do the research. It's a shame the only biographies of actors that we are exposed to are those who have been successful. It would be more instructive to talk to actors who never made a dime in the business. Because the public is usually exposed only to 'star' actors' lives, the idea of an actor's life is pretty much like what we see in the movies.

I have a friend who is a television editor. He has worked in the business all his life. Even so, he had never had an actor for a friend before we met. He was dumbfounded to find out all actors did not make the salaries reported in the newspapers. Nobody really wants to read that although an actor's minimum pay for a day on film is $448, he may not work more than two days per year, if that.

Acting is a profession. Any profession requires a big commitment. Years of study. Years of struggle. If your family is very wealthy, that may not be such a sacrifice.

The real challenge is not just doing without money, it's doing without validation. When your life is spent with people saying, '*No, thank you,*' all the time, it takes effort to stay positive.

Psychologists tell us that we get our picture of ourselves from our work. If you are not working, it's difficult to get a valid sense of self. The reality is that every actor spends more time unemployed than employed. Stardom is after all, only unemployment at a higher rate of pay.

The actor's life is very gruelling. For a long time, you may not be able to have a life other than pursuing work and when you finally do get work, your life will be working and pursuing work.

Choice of career is not just the choice of one's 9-5 endeavor, but the choice of lifestyle. Within the instability of the actor's life, it is difficult to plan for children, vacations, illness and other of life's other necessities, luxuries or surprises.

When you are unemployed, it's difficult not to be depressed and when you are working, there's little time for a mate and family.

So when you're available, you're depressed and when you're happy, you're unavailable. That can make an actor an undesirable mate. On the other hand, if you can remain balanced and remember that your mate and your kids are the ones who will be there for you when management won't, you can enjoy the luxury of time that periods of not working give you to be there when your kids get home from school, help them with their homework and to be there on a day to day basis for your mate. Then when you *do* work, your family will be able to enjoy your good fortune, confident that you will not go to work and forget to come home. They will know family life is the first priority.

Communication

So far, we haven't even dealt with the word communication. Most actors might not cite the need to communicate as their reason for getting into acting initially. Whether or not it is your goal, it's a natural offshoot of the process and thinking in these terms gives more weight to your endeavor and will help focus your goals.

It's easy to acknowledge the influence that writers can have on the public, but we tend to think of actors as merely delivering the writer's message. That's not entirely true. Roseanne Barr Arnold was a stand-up comedienne who wrote her own material when she created the character that has made her famous. That creation came out of what she communicated about being a working class wife and mother. If she had written this material for someone else, let's say Sally Field, (who also plays working class women) wouldn't Sally, just by being Sally, have made the theme a whole other thing? And if the producer had chosen Sally for the role of Roseanne, he would have been choosing Sally's trademark vulnerability instead of Roseanne's 'edge' and the same words would take on a completely different meaning.

Have you ever considered the 'message' you communicate by walking into a room? If you have on an Armani suit, people will not only get the idea that you have money, but that style and trend are very important to you. If you never comb your hair nor take a bath, you're definitely giving an antisocial message. It's not just our clothes, of course, it's our mannerisms and tone of voice and body language that communicate who we are.

I remember a conversation I had years ago with a friend of my daughter's. As a student at UCLA, she was appalled that another student had spit on her as she was sitting on campus. I agreed with her that just because her normal attire was green hair, clown white makeup and strange clothes, that did not give anyone the right to spit at her. I did point out to her, however, that it was not the sort of apparel that advertised her sociability. I mean, if you were lost and penniless on the subway platform, who would you be more prone to ask for help? I would approach the most respectable looking person there.

Check your message and make sure you are expressing your true voice. One of the problems with being trendy is that the meaning is generally:

I don't really have a message here, so I'm latching onto whatever is 'in' at the moment.

If you create a character and attend an audition in that guise, you are making a statement about how you see that character played. It may or may not be the same idea as the director, but you will have at least impressed him as someone who has a point of view and is not afraid to take responsibility for it.

Whether you are 'the good one', the 'bad one', the 'weird one', the 'banker', or 'the killer', the more identifiable you are as a 'something', the easier it will be for casting people to plug you into the system. The bad news, of course, is that you will feel type cast. We should all be so lucky. Worry about that *after* you are employed.

Burt Reynolds finally became famous because the nude centerfold he did in <u>Cosmopolitan</u> gave him the chance to announce who he was: a good-old-boy who could spoof himself and his masculinity with a sense of humor and still maintain his ability to kick butt. We look at Jane Fonda and we see a strong woman who stands tall for what she believes in. Sally Field's spunky little face personified courageous "Norma Rae" and before that, "The Flying Nun."

It's not that they got those parts and then that's what people saw them as. That's who they were. Sally Kirkland won an Academy Award nomination for being who she is. She probably never thought of her career as having to communicate something. She probably just thought she was looking for a job. In fact, that is a lot of what "Anna" was about.

The biggest break I ever had as an actress was my first film. In "Joe," I played the wife of a working man; a woman who was raised to say 'yes' and keep her man happy. I had been in training for years as a Catholic wife and mother.

Meryl Streep is a good example of someone who has played a wide variety of parts. She's the queen of characterization using different accents and wigs, body behavior and varied social class. The one thing that is common in her work is her intelligence. You have never seen Ms. Streep play someone who is dumb. Diane Sawyer is another persona that you look at and say 'smart'; Jane Fonda, 'strong'; Melanie Griffith, 'dumb like a fox'; Kevin Costner, 'all-American honesty'; Jack Nicholson, 'devilishly dangerous' and on and on. If you catch any of these performers on television in reruns of their early work, you will see the essence even then; time and experience has only honed that quality to it's most commercial aspects.

What Makes You So Special?

Let's focus on what about you is special. What do you want to say? You can't be someone who says, *I don't know,* when someone asks which restaurant you want to go to. You can't say, *I don't care,* when someone asks where you want to sit in the theater.

Have an opinion and know what you want. People should be able to answer a lot of questions just by looking at you. If you don't know the answer, you can't communicate it. They don't pay the big bucks for averageness, unless you are so average you can be the prototype, as Ron Howard was in "Happy Days." The people who will work in the business are those who can communicate a particular essence in the dramatic sense.

Elizabeth Dillon is a terrific acting teacher at

HB Studios in New York. She used to say that drama is heightened reality. Not just a sigh, but the most profound sigh. Not just a tear, but the most poignant tear. Not just a laugh, but a contagious laugh. The late New York agent, Michael Kingman says he seeks actors who have 'contagious emotions'.

Look in the dictionary. They say that dramatic is 'vivid,' 'startling,' 'highly effective,' 'striking.' Are you? You better not be just pretty. You better be beautiful. Pretty is a dime a dozen in the marketplace. You can even be ugly and have a career, but you better be *really* ugly. Phyllis Diller is an attractive woman, yet she made a career making us think of her as horse-faced. Whether you are extremely fat or extremely thin, you'd better have or create a look for yourself that is unique and then develop a persona to match it.

If you had been a friend of Danny Devito's, would you have foreseen his success? You probably would have, for he was part of an entrepreneurial group of actors in New York who produced their own material. A casting director might not have seen Devito's potential in a meeting, but watching him work could spark the c.d.'s imagination so that he could figure out a way to use him. The important part of the equation is that Danny had a vision of who he was and developed that by doing it. He did not wait to be chosen.

Being who you really are sounds easy, however most actors, have (unfortunately) spent a lifetime trying to become what they thought would please others (or at the other extreme, behaving badly, just for effect). The process of owning one's real feelings comes in fits and starts.

Do you prefer red or blue? Corduroy or

velvet? Rice Krispies or yogurt? How do you feel about gay people? Politics? Violence? What's your favorite music? Do you like candy? Do you eat meat? Are you formal? Casual? Flamboyant? Private? Do you even take the time to listen and find out the answers? Perhaps one of the answers is not to *do* so much: to listen more, to yourself as well as others.

Only when you have some of these answers do you have something to communicate. You will play many parts but it's your essence that makes the statement interesting - - or not.

I'm spending a lot of time talking about philosophy. That's appropriate since life is a mind-set. If you can conceptualize your goals accurately and specifically, you can plan a time-table and select a role model. The more precise your mind-set, the more efficient your efforts and the more fruitful your results.

Here are some more important questions for your notebook:

✓ Why do I want to act?
✓ Do I really want the life-style?
✓ What do I want to say?
✓ What makes me special?

Now, we're ready for the next step.

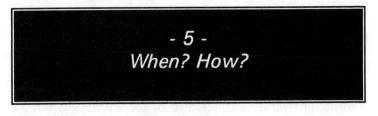

The dictionary says an actor is:

• *a person who acts in stage plays, motion pictures, television broadcasts, etc., esp. professionally.*

With that definition in mind, I have been an actor since I was five years old. That was when I was in my first play. The dictionary didn't say anything about tap dancing on Mona Ann Chadwick's front porch (which we did until the buses went by, since we were too embarrassed to have them see us) but I think that was acting, too. We are frequently destined to become actors well before we consciously make the commitment to making our living as performers.

Whenever civilians (people who are not 'in the business') come up to ask me questions about being an actress, they never ask a single question about how to act. Oh, some want to know how an actor remembers 'all those lines,' but they all seem to think that, of course, they would be able to act. They can easily conceptualize the process of enrolling in an acting school, but the thing that totally eludes them is how one translates acting ability into gainful employment. That concept also eludes many trained actors.

There is no big mystery. It simply entails being businesslike, focusing on a goal and marching toward it. Some people possess these skills naturally and others have to learn them. Some need to refine those skills, others just need support. The good news is that anyone can learn them.

From this point on in the book, you'll be given tasks to do. Finish the book first, so you will have the benefit of overview, then come back and begin your work.

Write Your Life Story

Get a pencil and an important book to write in; a scrap of paper is not enough; you are going into business so make sure your plans are stored appropriately. You will be referring to your notebook/journal frequently so make sure it is user friendly and reflects your style. Also you want it to bring a good price after you are famous and they auction it off.

Resist the temptation to use your computer or typewriter. There is a potent visceral force unleashed by the act of forming the words with your hands that takes thought one step closer to reality.

Write down all your best fantasies. They don't have to be realistic, but make sure they are attainable. You're not going to look like Tom Selleck, be ten years younger or a foot taller no matter how hard you work. Stick to the realms of possibility and probability. Do you want to win an Oscar? Own a Rolls? Speak French? Write it down. Live in the best part of town? Marry the person of your choice? Live happily ever after? Have 3 kids? No kids? Whatever. Think about it. Write everything down. You can edit later. Let yourself go.

Don't forget to write down what you are willing to do in return. Delay starting a family? Study? Be original? Unique? Find ways of doing things that no one has ever done before?

Goals

Do you want to be a classical actor? A commercial actor? An actor who does soaps? Film? Theatre? Do you intend to pursue your craft in your own smaller town? Do you intend to go 'big time' in Los Angeles or New York? Can you make a living as an actor in Rapid City, South Dakota? Can you make a living in show business in Wilmington, Delaware? Can you be happy with the options available to you in your own hometown?

If you live in a small town and your goal is to be a respected actor, your first goal might be some version of getting a part in a play. If there is not a theatre group, start one. If there is a theatre group, join it. Get a part if you can. If not, stage manage, help build sets, be the prop master, just become active and demonstrate your reliability and your creative powers in whatever job is available. Your time to act will come. You will figure out how to make it happen.

Whether or not we identify them as such, we set goals all the time anyway which I realized, recently, when I ran into an old college friend. He reminded me that in our first assignment in Public Speaking was to introduce yourself in some way to make people remember which one you were. I was alternately thrilled and mortified to hear him report that I had said:

I'm Kay Borman. You should remember my name because someday I am going to be famous and you are going to want to come swim in my swimming pool.

You know what? When I moved to New York to

finally seek fame and fortune, the subsidized low-income housing I lived in had a swimming pool and so does my home in California. From my Texas viewpoint, a swimming pool equated success as an actor. Since I was so powerful, I sure wish I had said:

Remember my name, I'm going to be the world's greatest actor and I will win five Oscars!

So as you conceptualize your goals, do yourself a favor: be informed and be specific. Focus on everything you want. If you commit to the goals, you will get them.

Immediate Goals

Your goal will obviously be intimately related to your marketplace. It's unlikely you'll be able to win an Oscar in Valentine, Nebraska. But you could probably have a career in local radio in Valentine.

Take the most important thing on your list. Let's say it is *win an Oscar.* Put a date on it. Say ten years from now. Then work backwards. What are the steps that would have to be taken before you could realize that goal?

Perhaps your list might look like this:

	Jan-Mar	April-June	July-Sept	Oct-Dec
Year 1	take acting classes/voice	join theatre company	get a part in a play research ad agencies for commercials	get your name in the paper re current project
Year 2	get a bigger part more press	do another play	explore book reviews	get Equity card
Year 3	get local commercial	more commercials	assemble an audition tape	explore stand-up
Year 4	move to LA or NY* get a place to live and make it wonderful	get an industry related job	get involved with theater company get pictures made	get a part in a play research casting directors
Year 5	get a commercial agent and get a commercial join SAG	get a part in a student or low budget film - add to audition tape start meeting casting directors	get another film part - revamp tape and start search for an agent get your name in the paper or do a radio interview	get a theatrical agent continue your agenting efforts - meeting casting directors, etc.

*Best time to move to Los Angeles is in August and
the best time to move to New York is in the Spring

And on and on. Make sure you leave a space to check off your goals as you achieve them. As you will notice, this is a five year plan. Set your own dates. If you manage to achieve some of these goals faster, fine, but this is a pretty realistic schedule. For every goal, focus on what you are willing to do to accomplish it: lose weight, learn to sing, get a second job, give up junk food, ask for what you want, etc.

If you wanted to build a house, it would be pretty clear that you would have to ask and answer a few questions. What kind of house do you want to build? Victorian? Modern? Country? What architect designs that type of house well? What type of building materials will you use? How much will it cost? Where will you get the money? What neighborhood do you want to build it in? What color will you paint it? Decorate it? Do you want to live in it for the rest of your life? Do you want to build it to sell? If so, there would be questions about what sells best, fastest, longest. You'd have to decide whether you want the *best* house in the world or whether you just want it built in a hurry in order to get a quick return on your investment.

In order to set goals for yourself as an actor, you'll need to answer similar questions to formulate a plan for success. Write about the life you want to lead: where you want to live it and what kind of house you want to live in. Describe the clothes you want to wear and the food you want to eat. Whether you want a cook or want to cook for yourself and your friends in a big family kitchen. Do you live alone? Are you married? Are you always involved with your current co-star? What? It's your story. No one else will read it.

Identify the roles you want to play. Discuss how you want a typical day in your life to be and visualize these goals on an emotional level. That is what engages the brain, focuses it and puts the plan into action.

Call this document "My Future." It should take at least two weeks to formulate. Remember, you are starting a business. Since you are investing your life in this pursuit, protect your investment by doing meticulous research and planning. The more you conceptualize acting as a business as well as an artistic venture, the more successful you can be. You will also be less likely to personalize the rejection.

Compose a short version detailing your current goals and what you are willing to do for it. Read it every day - first thing in the morning and last thing at night. You will experience your thought process beginning to change.

To give you support in focusing your goals, I recommend a terrific motivational tape (and there are many), "Think and Grow Rich" by Napoleon Hill. Hill is the original *positive thinking/you can do it* guru. He was saying things in 1937 that Anthony Robbins has enlarged upon today. Hill's message still packs a wallop and is a lot cheaper than the Robbins tapes. Robbins is equally effective and stimulating, so you can take your pick although I feel that Hill's is more altruistic.

Another inspiring book is "Wishcraft" written by Barbara Sher, published by Viking. The book goes into great detail about goal-setting.

I read that years before any kind of validation came their way, Sonny and Cher used to drive to Bel Air and sit in front of the gates of one of the swank- iest, most theatrically historic houses in town. They decided they would live in that house one day and they did.

Be Specific

Paul Linke, one of the stars of the hit series, "Chips" wrote a one man show about his own life called "Time

Flies When You Are Alive." In it, he told a wonderful story about being specific. He said he used to pray to get a part in a hit series and but for the omission of a single word: *quality*, he might have ended up on "Hill Street Blues" instead of "Chips."

I have my own specific story and it coincidentally involves an audition for "Hill Street Blues." The scene had to do with a woman who was hysterical because her no-good boyfriend had left her. I could not seem to find a way to motivate myself using that scenario. I could motivate myself substituting one of my kids for the love object. I reasoned, tears of rejection are tears of rejection. It worked. The scene went very well. Only one hitch. After my reading, the producer stopped me and said,

Could you do it again with a different thrust? That kind of seemed like one of your kids left you instead of your boyfriend.

They got it. They actually got what was going on in my mind although the words were totally different.

What a powerful weapon! You can have whatever you can imagine. Decide what you want. These decisions are not written in stone. You can change them. But the more detailed your life script, the less chance of error!!

Wouldn't it be interesting to know how Sonny and Cher got from sitting in front of the house to owning it? Do you suppose their first big goal was a hit record? Maybe the immediate goal was just to get to a place where they were hanging around with people in the business they could learn from. Perhaps their next goal was getting a paying job singing.

Targeting signposts that let you know you are

moving along will give you courage and inspiration when you need it most. When all seems dark, you can whip out your list and notice that, in fact, you have already accomplished A, B and C, even though D is eluding you at the moment. It's nourishing to notice when you make progress and celebrate it.

Support Groups

Find another ambitious actor to join you in your quest. You can be a team. Try for a team of four and make a commitment to support each other, meet twice a month to talk about your plans and announce your newest goal. Check each other to see that you are really staying on the track, making time tables and keeping on them. At each meeting, choose a new goal or take the last one further. There is something magic about saying your intention to another human being. The energy gets into the air and becomes concentrated and powerful.

Choose a role model. What actor/actress has the career and life you would like to have? You will have your very own one day, but today it will help you to have a concrete picture of your goal. Get a picture of your role model and put it where you will see it every day. If you have a hard time choosing a role model, this may be telling you something about your ambivalence about the business.

Go to the library. Ask the person at the reference desk all the sources for material written about your RM. Find out how he/she started and studied. If there's a biography, read it.

It's a good idea to give yourself the task of reading one show-biz biography every week. It is fascinating to find out how other people solved some of the same problems you have or will be faced with. It will be somewhat like inviting all those people over to brainstorm with you.

There are other practical nuts-and-bolts things we will talk about in the next chapter. For now, you have chosen your role model and I hope you've started a support group.

You can do all these things even before you study. Set study deadlines. Research the possibilities of teachers. Get a part-time job at a theatre or a radio or television station and see what it is really like.

Start at any point in your life. It may be five years before you can expect to realistically be looking for an actual part, but that's okay. Begin to conceptualize today.

Groundwork

In an actor support group that I belong to, an actor began lamenting pilot season. A pilot is the first show of a proposed television series. Getting a pilot, whether or not it is sold, can make an actor's year financially.

George was upset that he was not being sent on as many auditions as he felt he was due. He wondered what he could do to enhance his chances. The group concurred that the most important work toward getting a pilot comes 9 to 12 months prior to pilot season. Actors chosen for pilots are frequently those actors who have done other interesting (usually less lucrative) work all season that has gotten their agent and/or the casting director excited about submitting them for pilots.

You have to get the part before you can get the award. The most effective way to do this is to become an entrepreneur. If you're not going to do that, you must be very lucky. Many are. There's an old saying, *I'd rather be lucky than good.* Me, I would rather be lucky *and* good.

Let's talk a little about luck. It's very important to understand it. Yes, you can create your own luck. But even so, life really is like one big poker game. You are never going to get all winning hands and you won't get all losing hands either. The trick is to make the most of the wins while you minimize the losses. Learn to play poker well.

Burt Reynolds was one of the great box office draws for many years. His career has recently been on the ascendancy again because he now has a hit television series, "Evening Shade," but he is no longer, as they say in the business, 'hot' in films. Is it age? Or could it be that he is not as entrepreneurial as contemporary, Clint Eastwood, who still reigns at the movie box office. Clint has produced and directed many of his films. Two even more successful entrepreneurs are Sylvester Stallone and Arnold Schwarzenegger.

Positive Thinking

One of my favorite show business stories involves Eastwood and Reynolds. Once contract players for Universal, they were called in on the same day and told their contracts were not being renewed. Management said neither of them had a future. Reynolds, because he couldn't act, and Eastwood, because of his unusually large Adam's apple. As they were walking off together, lost in thoughts of failure, Reynolds turned to Eastwood and said:

Well, I can learn to act. What are you going to do?

We create our own lives. Successful people invent themselves.

Albert Hague was a Tony-winning composer before his success as an actor on the television show, "Fame." Since he had spent years 'on the other side of the table' watching actors make major audition mistakes, he used to run a very helpful class in auditioning for musicals.

I took that class early on in New York and although he had many valuable things to teach about auditioning and 'the business', the one quote that keeps coming back to me had nothing to do with career:

It takes a lot of creative energy to have an interesting life.

The real focus needs to be on your *life*. It can be as exciting as you are willing to create. With all the statistics and casualties and hard work, you *still* can be that actor who does work in the smallest or the largest marketplace.

Here are some more reminders for your notebook:

✓ make a specific plan
✓ set goals with date
✓ *consider what am I willing to do for it*
✓ make a commitment
✓ join or form a support group
✓ it takes lots of creative energy to have an interesting life

Your accomplishments all depend on how much time

and energy you are willing to expend, what you are *willing to do to accomplish your goals* and *how committed you are willing to be.* The next step is to organize yourself.

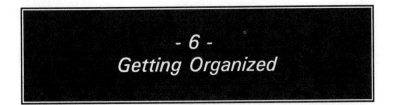

Your Ph.D.

Being an actor is like constantly pursuing a Ph.D.
The Ph.D. is a degree awarded for independent study.
Being an actor is all independent study.

It can get confusing and lonely pursuing something independently. It's hard to tell if you are making progress. There are so many possible ways to proceed, it is easy to get confused, run in many directions at once and accomplish nothing.

The one saving grace of being a candidate for the Ph.D. is you get to have a *major professor*. This is the person who discusses your goals with you, puts you on the right track and monitors your progress. Some major professors are better than others. As an actor, you will be your own major professor.

What a concept for an actor. Since we are in the habit of playing parts anyway, if we conceptualize a part of ourselves as the MP, we can slip into character, become wise and perhaps even gain perspective.

I do a version of it all the time. I say,

Gee, if I were a character in a play, what would I do in this situation?

Sometimes when I can't figure out what to wear or combine with something, I will just say, and somehow I make the right choice. Just like air-conditioning, I don't know why it works, it just does.

First Things First

•*Get a job and a nice place to live. Truthfully, you would be amazed. People take years to take care of that problem. In New York, especially, it's so important to have a base. One of our clients said in an interview recently that acting wasn't her life. Her life was her life. Acting was what she did. She loved doing it and didn't want to do anything else. But it wasn't her life.*

Whenever people said they were having problems with their acting and what could they do to change it, her response was always, 'change your life.' That's something young actors don't want to believe, but I think it's very true.

So if I just arrived in New York, I wouldn't worry so much about acting until I solved the problem of where I was going to live, how I was going to make a living and how I was going to get by day-to-day because I don't think you can solve anything else first.
Tim Angle, Agent
Triad Artists, New York

If you are still in your own hometown, you probably have already taken care of this. You may still live with your folks or you may already have your own place. The important thing is to establish a base of operations. Make your space as comfortable, light and inviting as possible for yourself. Your nest also needs to be organized and private.

It can be pretty debilitating to be self-employed. Nothing demands our attention at a particular moment. We could sleep until noon if we chose. There's no place we have to be at a particular time. In the abstract, this might sound like heaven. In reality, it can be pretty depressing.

The structure of a regular job demands some sort of mental health. There are times set for arriving, eating, leaving. There are tasks to be performed, people to talk to, people to rebel against, someone to pay us. There's frequently some type of dress code. Become self-employed or in the case of the actor, self-employed/unemployed and the situation is a real challenge.

Work Corner

Establish a work center that includes your desk, Rolodex, phone, answering machine, book shelves with room for a good reference library, plus storage space for all your office supplies, pictures, resumes, manila envelopes, mailing labels, typewriter, good stationery and good lighting.

You need a clock and a pad and pencil for messages by the telephone. There should be a pencil and pad next to *every* telephone in your house. Never keep any business contact waiting on the phone while you search the house for pencil and paper.

Don't use this space (even if it is just a corner of your kitchen or bedroom) for anything but work. Then your unconscious will subtly begin to shift into business/creative mode every time you sit at your desk. I have a favorite chair I have endowed as my 'inspiration chair' and I sit in it every time I read a script and prepare for an audition. I have called it my

magic chair and fully expect to have great inspiration
every time I sit there. It usually works for me in a
way no other space in my house does.

Looking For Work

Looking for work is our main job as actors. It is
stressful to be constantly rejected, like being continually exposed to a virus, pretty soon it wears down
the system. In order to counteract that, it's important
to control all the things we can control. The
familiarity of our routine will soften the effects of
never knowing when we will be making money again,
so make a list of things you are going to do daily. Set
aside specific times for each of these activities and
stick to it.

Familiarity Breeds Comfort

Schedule a time for awakening and going to bed. You
don't have to be fanatical about it, but the more you
adhere to a schedule, the more secure you will feel.
We are all comforted by the familiar. There is enough
in the actor's life that you can't control so take charge
of the things you can. It will make a difference.

Schedule errands for one particular day of the
week and put a time frame around them. These tasks
have a way of eating up time. No matter how oner-
ous, they are a lot more fun than calling up some
person who might end up saying 'no' to whatever we
are asking.

My son-in-law says, errands are those things
we do when we're not doing what we are supposed to
do. I agree.

Spiritual and Physical Health

No matter what, exercise daily and eat nutritiously. If you begin each day with stretching and exercise, you can assist your body's own natural resistance to both physical and emotional illness while keeping your instrument fit and in tune. Get sufficient sleep. If you feel yourself beginning to get depressed, check to see if these basics are taken care of.

It is important to take time for a regular-sit-down-meal. And even if you can't resist eating self-destructively, counter that behavior by detoxifying your system as much as possible with good food along with it. The famous nutritionist, Dr. Henry Beiler declares that green vegetables (the darker green the better) detoxify the system.

Students at The American Conservatory Theater in San Francisco have told me when Los Angeles' famous nutritionist, Eileen Poole visited regularly on a volunteer basis to advise the students on appropriate eating habits, that she was so inspirational that the students actually gave up sugar and caffeine. One of those students, actress Annabella Price, told me that her mental outlook as well as her physical abilities improved dramatically.

We already discussed forming a support group for acting goals. It's even more important to have a regular family experience to support your personal life. If you don't have a family nearby, form one with members of your acting class or your neighbors or the people from the laundromat. The operative words here are 'create a family for yourself.' I believe one of the great lures of being an actor is the 'families' we create when we work.

In his book, "The Right Place at the Right

Time," employment consultant Dr. Robert Wegmann states:

• *To help maintain perspective: Exercise regularly...and keep in close contact with friends whom you trust and with whom you can share your experiences.*

Life is problem solving and that's a lot easier to solve with the support of loved ones. It helps immensely to be involved regularly with a group of people who acknowledge this, offer mutual support and encourage shared feelings.

The 12-step groups are fabulous (Alcoholics Anonymous, Overeaters Anonymous, Adult Children of Alcoholics, etc.). They boil down to free group therapy any day of the week and a family support group.

When we join existing support groups, we are usually in a vulnerable state and we are ready to lay down all our defenses in the hopes of feeling better. I'm not against that in concept, but retain your own persona and way of speaking. Don't throw out the baby with the bath water.

Some people go to church. Others practice Yoga, the martial arts, or gardening. Choose whatever might get you in touch with your own vitality. You will be stronger, more vulnerable and a better actor. The added self-esteem will help put your career in perspective.

Time Out

There are all kinds of meditation. I don't care which kind you choose, but it is vital to take 10-20 minutes twice a day to for yourself. To take stock. To be silent. No music. No eating. No drinking. No talking. Just to be with yourself. Not just when you think about it or if it happens, but a regularly scheduled time for you and yourself. Many people believe these are the moments that allow you to tune in to your own feelings and intuitions. If you get too busy to do that, you are too busy.

Class/Study/Teachers/Gurus

When I lived in New York, I went to dance clases three times a week, a voice lesson once a week and worked with an accompanist one other day of the week. I was also in an acting class one night a week. Depending on your goals, you should be involved in some version of this. Classes not only improve our skills, but they keep us involved with people, plugged into the net-work of actors and help structure our days.

A word here about teachers. I think most of us are looking for 'the secret of life,' 'the answer,' the 'magic ingredient' that is going to make life work better. And really, I think actors believe in magic more than most people so I caution you, if you can find a great teacher to work with in Podunk, New York or Hollywood, do it. There are wonderful teachers out there who can help us marshal our forces, *but* do not give up your own thought processes. Even very good and very reputable teachers sometimes have their own agenda. Perhaps it is religious or political or just simply 'getting laid', but that is their agenda, not yours.

Since people are defined by their belief systems, don't allow anyone to trivialize yours.

Refine them as you grow, but question, question, question. You don't have to be a pain in the butt about it and do it out loud, but a certain amount of skepticism is healthy. As an actor, all you have to sell is your *self*, so make sure it's still in tact when class is over. Don't blindly follow anyone.

Acting is greatly entwined with our psychological well-being. That doesn't mean making our psyches vulnerable to just anyone who displays an interest. If you need help, get a reputable shrink and deal with your emotional problems there. Don't let acting teachers play in your mind.

If a teacher is opposed to anyone with other thought processes, watch out. If you stay with people who do not encourage you to question, how will you ever nurture your imagination and exercise your own creativity? Give yourself credit. A friend of mine left her acting class not long ago when the teacher declared:

You have really become a better actor since you began working with me.

My friend had not had a job during the entire time she had been in class.

Focused Analytical Viewing

Study covers a host of subjects beside formal classes in acting, camera skills, etc. Your education in this field includes viewing the work of *anybody* who is doing the job you want and analyzing what makes him good at his job. Or what is lacking.

It really is not helpful (to you or anyone else) to say,

I hated that movie.

That play was no good.

That actor stinks.

Helpful is:

The movie moved too slowly and was not focused.

The play didn't work for me because the lead was miscast. It required someone more flamboyant.

Gee, she's usually so good. It's good to remember that we can all be bad. I wonder what happened.

Begin to think in a problem-solving way. Not only will you be more interesting to be around since you will be looking for a solution, but you'll never be bored and you will find that your own work will improve.

Your Laboratory

As part of your education as an actor, get a job working in the business in some area other than acting. Be an usher in the theater or work in an agent's office or a radio station. Be a 'go fer'. You will begin to get a clearer idea of what is entailed in the lifestyle. It may not be as appealing up close. If that is the case, think of all the time and heartache you have saved yourself.

When I was interviewing agents for *The New York Agent Book,* I met a young woman who was assisting a famous agent. An aspiring actress, she had come to New York from a small town. After spending two years seeing first hand *how it really is*, she no longer wants to be an actress. She now perceives the life style as too depressing and it no longer appeals to her. She now wants to be a producer and have power and a decent life style.

Read Show Business Books

Read books about the business and what it's really like. Books I recommend for this are:

A Book/Desi Arnaz
Acting with a Passion/Allan Miller
Adventures in the Screen Trade/William Goldman
Audition/Michael Shurtleff
Final Cut/Steven Bach
Indecent Exposure/David McClintock
Just One More Time/Carol Burnett
Reel Power/Mark Litwak
Saturday Night Live/Doug Hall - Jeff Weingrad
The Season/William Goldman
You'll Never Have Lunch
      in This Town Again/Julia Phillips
Wired/Bob Woodward

There are many others. These are just ideas for a starting library. Schedule time each day for business-related reading. Whether this means gleaning your local newspaper for announcements of play auditions, noticing who just took over an ad agency or when the local Lion's Club might need a speaker. Do it regularly.

Money Wisdom/Negotiating Savvy

There's no guarantee that even if you get a prestigious acting job that you will still be able to pay your rent. Off Broadway and chorus jobs don't pay much and decent showcases (which there is great competition for) don't pay anything at all. And sometimes, when you do get a job paying a lot of money, that can end up being a trap. It's very seductive to work every day and make good money. If you are on a soap opera or a television series, you are lucky enough to be employed for several years, but you only get to play one role. Many actors in this position have yearned to leave those jobs for what they felt would be more 'artistically challenging work', but the money makes any artistic decision hard to make.

Other actors, who do not have as *visible* nor lucrative careers are frequently more fulfilled though much less regularly employed because they have the opportunity to play more varied parts.

Though actors who are currently making money refuse to believe it, money seldom continues in an unbroken string. It's never wise to live up to ones highest earning level without providing for the day when those bucks either shrink or disappear completely.

The third year after I arrived in New York, I made a lot of money in commercials. When I visited my accountant, he cautioned me about changing my life style.

• *It won't last. Take your children on trips and enjoy it, but don't get a new apartment. I prepare actor's income tax returns all the time. It won't last.*

I'm very conservative anyway, so I provided for myself but I secretly thought he was wrong. I was different. I was just going to make *more* money every year. Sure!! Only two years later my income was only one third of what it had been.

Pretty humbling but you know what? When I get on a string of work - I *still* think there will be no more dry seasons. Hope springs eternal!

During that flush time, I had dinner one night with the producer of the soap I was guesting on. The real purpose of the dinner was for the producer to ascertain whether or not I was interested in joining his show as a regular before he would go back, find a place for me and make a real offer. In my first two years in the city, I dreamed of such a job, but by the time of that dinner, I was already making enough money via commercials. The idea of being tied to a soap no longer appealed to me.

The producer wanted his information from the dinner and I wanted mine. I was curious to know how well my agent had negotiated for me. I had no meter to measure whether the money she got for me was good, better, best.

The producer did me a big favor. He not only answered my question honestly, but he gave me a little education as well:

• *Part of being an actor is having that information yourself. You have to tell your agent what to ask for. You have to know what people are getting paid. You must know all the business ramifications as well.*

From that day forward, I've always talked to other actors about money. I have all the manuals available from each of the unions detailing pay scales. I make it a point to share information regarding what I am making and what others in the marketplace are making. If an actor never knows that his peers are capable of getting $1500 or more for a day of work, he will never press for it.

Enhancing the Merchandise

Another part of your education includes knowing everything required to make you look good. It seems pretty astounding that the only people Cher thanked when she won her Academy Award were her make-up and hair people, but a large part of Cher's appeal is her visual impact. She's pretty open about her plastic surgery; this is a woman who invented herself. Within her single-minded focus on herself, she breathes so much energy that it emanates from her constantly in the form of charisma.

Successful movie stars understand everything about how they are lit in a scene and they know about camera angles. If you plan to make your living in front of a camera, get a camera and photograph everybody you know. Look at the photos intently. Study why one is more appealing than another. Get your own video camera and set it up and photograph yourself. Do a scene and see how your face looks from different angles or in different light.

A story that demonstrates how successful this approach can be involves Sara Purcell, currently starring on "The Home Show." The road to that success was predictable, if you knew Sara and her now ex-husband, Joe. While working in a department store in San Diego, she got a chance to audition to be one of the hosts for a local talk show in Los Angeles called "AM/Los Angeles." She found out on Friday about the audition for the following Monday. Luckily, she was married to a man who directed local television commercials and is enormously creative, talented, supportive and owned a video camera in a time when most folks didn't.

All weekend they taped Sara interviewing their friends. They would tape, then sit back, look and critique. What worked? What didn't? How did she look when she moved a lot? A little? What was visually interesting? Everything, I guess for Sara not only got the job, but after a few years spent interviewing on AM/Los Angeles, she moved onto the network with "Real People" and all the work that followed.

Besides being very smart and enormously resourceful, Sara also has an innate sense of fun that's always apparent in her work. Those are the traits that she has enlarged upon to become a performer with a consistently successful track record.

The stars I know have dedicated themselves *single-mindedly* to their careers. Are you prepared to do that?

Male actors (and actually male superstars in every business) frequently have a much easier time concentrating on themselves. Our culture expects this and many women (me included) want to nurture and support the people in their lives. That support adds energy to the project and energy sent forth in a concentrated manner always brings results.

Relationships

Don't forget about the people in your life. Actors have a reputation for being totally self-involved. It's hard not to be. We have to sell ourselves; assess where the next job is coming from; permit our uniqueness; and deal with how our changing physicality is affecting our marketability. So sometimes, we can get engrossed in ourselves and miss out on the really important things in life; family and friends. It takes creative energy to live a balanced life, it doesn't just happen.

When I started in the business in New York, my children were young. Everyday, they waited anxiously for me to get home. They wanted to tell me everything about their day. They wanted to tell me who hit who. They wanted hugs and kisses. After a day out making rounds, all I really wanted to do was come home, get my messages, have a Dr. Pepper, go to the bathroom and relax.

Of course, I couldn't. They needed me. But, I couldn't really give them my undivided attention because I needed some time to myself. I hit upon what we called 're-entry time'. Kids can understand anything if you are straight about it. I explained I needed 15 minutes when I first got home to deal with all phone calls, mail, etc.

When I got home they headed straight for the kitchen timer, set it for 15 minutes and when the bell rang, I had 're-entered the atmosphere' and was ready to give them my absolute attention. Actually, re-entry time turned out to be a pretty viable concept for all our relationships and each of us has incorporated 're-entry time' into our lives to this day. There is a way to tend to business *and* pleasure.

All we have is today. Since all the really successful people say the most fun was 'getting there,' make sure you and your family enjoy the trip.

Some more things to add to your notebook:

✓   get a job
✓   organize personal life
      get apartment
      make a schedule
      create and set aside workspace
✓   physical and spiritual health
✓   provide for emotional needs; friends
✓   professional support group
✓   get in classes
✓   get a teacher not a guru
✓   retain belief systems
✓   practice informed viewing
✓   get a job in the business
✓   read books about the business
✓   be wise about money
✓   learn union minimums and how to negotiate
✓   enhance the merchandise
✓   nurture your relationships

Now, let's talk about the product.

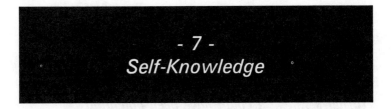

An entrepreneur is someone who organizes, manages and assumes responsibility for a business. The most important considerations to his business are his product and how he markets it.

When I was interviewing agents for *The Los Angeles Agent Book* and *The New York Agent Book*, I always ended the meeting with the same question:

What don't actors know?

The answer was invariably the same:

Themselves.

• *Successful actors have an accurate image of what they sell. Unsuccessful actors don't have an accurate image of what they sell. That's the sign. If you're going out and you're getting the job, then you know who you are. If you're going out and you're not getting the job, then something is wrong. And you can't say it's talent. In this town, talent doesn't mean a lot. If you are the right type, you will get the job. I'm not saying you are going to get "Hallmark Hall of Fame," signed contract, but you will be getting work.*
> Martin Gage, Agent
> The Gage Group, Los Angeles

His East Coast counterpart, Phil Adelman had another way of saying it:

• I had a funny-looking lady come in, mid-30's, chubby, not very pretty. For all I know, this woman could be brilliant. I asked her what roles she could play; what she thought she should get. She saw herself playing Debra Winger's roles. Kathleen Turner's roles. I could have been potentially interested in this woman in the areas in she would work. But it was a turn-off because, not only do I know that she's not going after the right things, so she's not preparing correctly, but she's not going to be happy with the kinds of things I'm going to be able to do for her. So I wouldn't want to commit to that person.

Martin added:

• You must always show the most commercial quality. They may or may not be buying it that day, but one day they will and they will have already seen the one person who could do this better than anyone else in the world.

But how do you go about finding out which one you are?

That's not going to happen overnight. It takes time to become, to develop your own flavor. You must study. Not just acting. Go to the museum. Learn how the masters perceived love, anger, despair. The more you perfect your own persona and trust your instincts, whether it is for what constitutes a really great pair of socks or a superb jump shot, the more you become the one you are. Have the awareness to get it.

When I first arrived in New York, I did everything I could to prevent being mistaken for a 'middle-class Lady-from-Texas' (which I was). I wanted so badly to be a 'classy New York Lady.' I didn't realize (Texas accent notwithstanding) my very middle-classness is what I had to sell. Yes, I can (and have) played ladies who went to Vassar, but they can (and will) *get* a lady from Vassar for those parts. I'm an authentic woman from Texas who has raised kids and has all those other unique things that come with my persona. And there is nobody else who has all these components. My goal is to finally get comfortable with my *self* and endeavor to tie that uniqueness to a universality of the life experience.

All the time I was in New York, when I thought I was fooling everyone into thinking I was a sophisticated Vassar-type lady, I was always cast as the same middle-class person I am. When I arrived in Los Angeles, I had more or less accepted myself in that light. So, naturally, it has been in Los Angeles where I have been given the opportunity to play society ladies, sophisticated lesbians, bitches and a whole wonderful spectrum of different roles.

Getting To Know You

Los Angeles agent Martin Gage (an ex-actor) has some insights regarding self-discovery:

• *Anything you can do to give you more of an idea who you are, whether it's therapy, talking to people, to looking in a mirror, that's valid.*

There's an exercise I used to give my class when I taught actor therapy. I would tell them to get stark naked in front of a mirror and sit and look at themselves for an hour. Just sit and look at yourself. Talk to yourself. Look at how you look when you talk.

When you cross your legs. When you move. Look at how your face changes. Look at how your body moves.

Think of all your competition. Think of what is unique about each of them. Think about what is different in you that is not in them. Watch what you do with your hands. Watch yourself. See yourself. You may have to do it for a year. For three weeks. Who knows for how long until all of a sudden you see something that is accessible that people will buy. The smart actor will study himself until he can see 'what it is that I have that is unique, special, commercial, saleable, acceptable in me that I can develop and magnify and use better than anybody else.'

Think of you and your four closest competitors. If someone sat and talked to each of you for 20 minutes, what would they see that was different? What is it about you? Why should they hire you instead of the other one? She may have more credits or make more money. Why should I hire you? You have to go in with the qualities that are the most accessible of you to make those people buy you.

When you walk in a room, you have about four seconds while people decide to hire or not hire you. It's your vibes. They may call it your nose, but it's your vibes. You have to go in with the qualities that are the most accessible of you. You've got to get those people to buy you.

> Martin Gage, Agent
> The Gage Group, Los Angeles

John Kimble, partner at one of Los Angeles' prestigious conglomerate star agencies, supports Gage's thesis.

• *I believe every person on the face of the earth is unique. I believe that if I had a set of identical twins who were in touch with their uniqueness, I could sell them separately because, once they are in touch with their own uniqueness, there is no such thing as competition. If you are in control of your uniqueness and you are centered, you take that into a room and if someone chooses not to use it, you can't feel negative. It simply meant they didn't want to use that uniqueness. You are not in competition with anybody else.*

A person's ideas dictate his uniqueness. What I believe about homosexuality or what I believe about any major subject is my 'unique' because it comes from my experience of it. So you can't compare it. Many times you will be in the minority. The greatest people in the world have normally been in the minority.

John Kimble, Agent
Triad, Los Angeles

• *This is what I am. This is what they want me to be. Can I put them together and find out what I am capable of being. They want me to be a nerd. I want to be sexy. Maybe I can be a sexy nerd. Then you have to convince your agent that that's what you are, because if your agent doesn't see it, you're out again. If the agent sees you and thinks he can make money on you, but not in the same way you think, then you have a problem. You and the agent must have the same vision. You might change his vision or he might change yours. If you both have the same vision, you'll be successful. The level of success may vary, but if you know who you are and the agent knows it, accurately, that's the recipe for success.*

And remember, what you are at 25 is not what you are at 35. Things change and your perception of yourself must change, too.

Martin Gage, Agent
The Gage Group, Los Angeles

Martin said the key words on the previous page: develop and magnify. In the film, "Stage Door,' you have the opportunity to see several actresses at the beginning of their careers before they 'developed and magnified' their respective 'uniquenesses'. It's fascinating to see Kathrine Hepburn, Lucille Ball, Eve Arden and Ginger Rogers in such an early stage of development. Perhaps these ladies are not as familiar to you as other later day actors you routinely see on television, but if you do know their later work, here is an opportunity to see several actors in one sitting and glean the kernal of what became their ticket to stardom. It's a very instructive process.

Other Factors

• *The actor has got to have the creative energy juices flowing and have the right mind-set and the right attitudes to have the wins come to him. He needs to have an angle on the role that's going to be different and maybe the director is going to say,* That's *interesting. If the actor is not in his most creative time, he's going to miss some things. He's going to walk out of the audition and say, 'Damn, I should have put this twist on it,' or 'I don't know why I did that: it's so obvious.'*

If an actress' energies are in the theatre, and she hasn't done a play in a year, it's going to drain her and she needs to be filled up and dealing with what to do about that. Equity Waiver, scene study, comedy workshop. There are lots of choices; not just sit home and stare at the bare walls.

> Ann Geddes, Agent
> Geddes Agency, Los Angeles

Dan Faucci, vice-president of comedy development at Paramount pictures, told me that when he was an actor, he used to meet with two other actors three times a week for two hours to work on camera reading commercial copy and evaluating each other. I asked him if it helped him and if he began booking jobs. His answer:

• *Yes. We did book jobs, but I think it didn't matter whether or not we had the camera. It was the fact that we met three times a week focusing on what we wanted.*

He also taught me a terrific exercise. Spend 10 minutes communicating with yourself in the mirror. Do it by the clock. Just look at your face. Don't look for anything. You can look at your eyes, nose, lines, skin. See what you focus on. Don't judge it. Experience it. Take it in. If you start getting itchy at eight minutes, you're probably getting ready to feel something that is beginning to make you uncomfortable, be brave: spend the full time and see what feelings come up.

Assets and Liabilities

Make a list of all your skills. Your acting-related skills, your entrepreneurial skills, everything you do well. Include making friends and staying positive if that's in your repertoire. These insights may take you further in your exploration.

How you work on the tasks we are speaking of delineates who you are. Your whole life is a laboratory to keep on looking at your way of working. If you procrastinate about your pictures and resumes, you are going to procrastinate about learning your lines.

Napoleon Hill in his book "Think and Grow Rich," says that every person has to conquer procrastination. Start now to do all your tasks the moment you think of them. As you work on the details of any project, you will work on every facet of your life. Begin to practice what you want your life to be.

I love what a friend of mine told me about taking workshops. He said that if he takes a workshop or a class, he is determined to get something out of it:

If I pay my money to be transformed, I'm going to be transformed.

I feel the same way. If I'm going to expend energy, I want something back out of it. I don't want to be in an acting class where I only get to work once in six weeks.

Make a list of your liabilities. As you list drawbacks, perhaps you can formulate a plan to overcome them. If you think they're unsolvable problems, read Carol Burnett's biography. There's no one in this business who could have been more disenfranchised than she was. If she could become successful against those odds, believe me, you have a chance *if* you can become that focused.

Hector Elizondo (who has worked for years, but finally became "visible" as the hotel manager in

"Pretty Woman") is a very successful actor who has interesting things to say about hardship:

- *You can't really have style unless you've been someplace. I mean, you have to have been down. You have to have overcome something to have something. If you've had everything all your life, then you've never been tested and I don't think you're really the genuine article.*

  You have to have come through something - because that's how a sword is made. It's made from a piece of iron from the ground, and it's forged and beaten - that's the great metaphor for a human being. If you're born a sword, you aren't a real sword. But if you're forged from this iron ore - then comes this beautiful sword.
  "From 'Pretty Woman' to Plenty Busy" -
  Elias Stimac
  Drama-Logue
  Sept 19-25, 1991

It's entirely possible that you have to come from a background of great pain to have that kind of drive. I contend that a balanced person would not have the drive to be a star in any field because he would not have that desperate need to prove himself

Focusing On What You Have To Sell

Knowing what you have to sell does not necessarily mean always preparing yourself to play the same part, but preparing to focus on the essence that will alert the casting director to your strength. If you consistently play banker types, it's probable that you have a innate fastidiousness that is associated with 'detail-oriented' people. If you exaggerate and develop this trait, you might be the first thought for any casting executive who is casting these roles.

The question of style is an integral part of the "who am I?" equation. Martina Navratilova is never going to hit the ball the way Chris Evert does. They each have an innate style borne of their unique backgrounds. Sylvester Stallone and Arnold Schwarzenegger are both strong men, but Stallone's style is totally different than Schwarzenegger's. Think about them a moment and characterize what is different about each and why you would cast one in one project, but what you would have to change if the other actor was chosen.

Analyze the people in your acting class. Try to perceive what they have to sell, not just what part they should play. What are their strengths and weaknesses? After you've seen them work two or three times, try to imagine how they are going to approach their next scene. Will they use their forehand or backhand? The more you are able to examine others, the more per-fected that skill becomes for your own use.

Once you begin to successfully isolate your strengths and develop them, these attributes will take on a life of their own. There is an esoteric law of attraction: focus on your goal, do your work, live your life, the goal becomes yours.

Mentors/Role Models

Don't you envy those people who appear to have mentors while you are slugging away doing all the work alone? If you want a mentor, go get one. Choose someone whose work and/or life you admire and cultivate a relationship. You find someone who has what you want and you ask them questions. Not everyone will cooperate, but some will. Readers call me all the time asking me questions about agents. I always help them. My friends have warned:

You're going to be sorry. Everyone is going to take advantage of you.

They're wrong. It's mainly the winners who are smart enough to figure out how to call me. They don't whine and they are careful not to waste my time. They all have plans. And I (just like everyone else) love the opportunity to share what I know.

Mentors and role models can be quite helpful over the course of your life, but again, keep the skepticism meter handy. You don't want to *become* the mentor or role model, you just want to profit from their wisdom and encouragement. You can't have a mentor or a career if you are afraid to ask. Focus on your goal. Greet every experience as though you were going to have to write a paper on it. It will keep you focused and in the present. Say to yourself before every meeting, even lunch with your friend,

What do I want from this experience?

Lunch and to energize my friendship.

If we all took the time to consciously think of such goals before our actions, we'd be less likely to get off the track, take a disagreement personally and get bogged down in negativity. If the goal is to make things work, not to be *right*, make points, or show someone the error of his ways, things do work and everyone has better time.

Business Relationships

• *Besides working on your acting, which should be a constant, study the business and get to know how it works. Get involved in the community and don't only get involved with other actors. Get to know the rest of the creative community. Try to maintain relationships at higher levels. It's a business.*

    Barry Freed, Agent
    The Barry Freed Company
    Los Angeles

• *An actor should work on his energy. A lot of times when actors go in to meet producers and directors, they get so nervous. Don't be desperate, be happy that you have the interview. If you're right for the part, you'll get it.*

    Rickey Barr, Agent
    Rickey Barr Talent Agency
    Los Angeles

• *It's also a question of the competition. You can send a girl in who's very pretty, does a great reading, but somebody else will come in that happens to be a friend of the producer or a nephew of the director or somebody that somebody wants to go to bed with. Or whatever. There's 20,000 reasons why you're not going to get the part. And it's not necessarily that you are without talent. It's because there is so much competition. When I think about it, when I look at the end of the week and I see all the people I've gotten out on appointments, I say to myself, 'It's amazing that I did that. I'm just one little person.' When I think about all the agents and all the actors, I think we're lucky to*

get people out on the appointment.
> Elinor Berger, Agent
> The Irv Schecter Agency
> Los Angeles

• *Look at yourself very carefully and see what's being bought at the time; what actors are doing most of the work. If actors see it clearly, they can see if they fit into a niche in the business. Maybe, agewise, they have to grow into a character. But don't stick around Hollywood while that's happening. Don't be available for one or two lines, one scene. Get out and refuel yourself as an actor. Do it somewhere. I know it's very difficult to give up home and family and go off into the hinterlands and work, but there's got to be some pride there.*
> Alex Brewis, Agent
> Brewis Agency, Inc.
> Los Angeles

The most important part of this quote is *...and see what's being bought at the time.*

In situation comedies, there is usually a next door neighbor (man, woman or both) who is zanier, less pretty/handsome than the lead. Frequently there is an acerbic, scratchy quality to contrast the lead.

The lead needs to be more bland than the supporting players in order to create the perfect balance. When you make a cake, flour (bland) is the chief ingredient followed in quantity (but not importance) by the liquid (the binder) and the spices. The flour holds it all together and the spices add zip, but too much vanilla or sugar or salt (without which the project or cake would be inedible) would render the effort useless as well. "Barney Miller" worked because Hal Linden was so bland. Mary Tyler Moore waited many years to win an Emmy until almost every other actor on the show had been rewarded because no one was able to realize the contribution of her steadiness. It's instructive and comforting to notice these stock components in every genre.

In adventure/detective shows, there's usually a hard-boiled chief that is at odds with the hero. And of course, there are always exotic BAD guys and white trash bad guys and corporate bad guys. If you can come up with a new twist on the bad guy, you can really be in demand. Commercials feature the dumb one (with the problem) and the smart one (who solves the problem).

The large marketplace is constantly changing and the smaller marketplaces usually follow that lead a year or two down the road.

When I was working on "It's a Living," I had a conversation with Ann Jillian. As you probably recall, she had a mastectomy a few years ago. During chemotherapy she amassed a wardrobe of wigs which she maintains to this day because she feels it very necessary to look exactly the buyers expect her to look:

• *Once you are lucky enough to establish an image, it's important to keep it.*

Knowing When To Change

The search for our professional identity is an ongoing process. And it changes. Does anybody remember that Donna Mills' image used to be the 'passive, adorable, trustworthy blonde' instead of the 'evil, spiteful and conniving Abbey' she became on "Knots

Landing?"

Donna decided that she wanted that part and went for it. David Jacobs, producer of "Knots," told me her agent called and wanted her considered for the part. Her agent was told:

Okay, we know Donna. We'll consider her.

No, no, retorted Donna's agent. *She wants to come in and read for the part.*

The producers were blown away by the reading. In fact, their idea of Donna's image at that time would have kept them from seriously considering her for the part.

Calling and insisting to be read was a very 'Abbey' thing to do. Abbey was a lady who got what she wanted. It isn't just that Donna put on more exotic make-up and turned into Abbey. Obviously, her adjustment to life changed, too.

It's Never Over

Happily, it's never over. We don't ever finish learning to act. I wonder if any professional ever finishes studying. A brain surgeon learns a particular procedure one day, but if he doesn't continually practice and refine the technique, he won't be the brain surgeon everyone wants. If he does not continue to read, search and study, he will not maintain his superiority. Neither actor nor surgeon will prosper without enjoying and practicing the continuity of process.

I sat in on a class of well-regarded director and acting teacher, Milton Katselas. A working actor said he had to keep it together a little longer because he knew *the payoff* was just around the corner. Milton stopped him and asked,

What's just around the corner?

The payoff, the actor responded.

No, Milton countered,

The payoff is now.

All we have is now. If you are not fulfilled by the now, get out of the business. If the payoff for you is a Tony, an Oscar, or big bucks, change jobs now. You will miss your whole life waiting for the prize. If you are unfortunate enough to get the prize while in this mind-set, you will find you are the same unhappy person you were the day before you got your statue.

I once heard an interview on the radio with Desi Arnaz, Jr, a young actor who 'had it all' for all intents and purposes. He said:

• *Yes, it did seem like I 'had it all'. Except that's not 'it.' I had the car, the house, the position and I was terribly unhappy. I got into alcohol and drugs. That wasn't 'it' either. There's really no difference between me and the people who have nothing...who think 'it' is all those things. They, at least, think if they had a big career and all the things money can buy, they would be happy. Imagine how depressing it is to have all those things and still be unhappy?*

It's up to you and how smart you are, how you make positive choices, how you focus, how you ask for what you want, how you don't let yourself sink into negative thinking. It's absolutely self indulgent to allow yourself to think:

Oh, I'll never get a job.

Oh, I'll never get a job again.

Nobody wants me.

I'm no good.

Not only does nobody want to hear you talk like that and/or be around you in that frame of mind, but that thinking only drains your energy and prolongs your pain. Don't cut yourself off from your feelings (you don't have to go into denial) go ahead and acknowledge the pain and then go for a walk. Spend time with yourself. Explore. Use the meditation time I spoke about to just 'be'. Gain perspective. This business is a constant test for maintaining perspective.

Do a lot of writing. Writing is a magical exercise. At my most depressed moments, when I can remember to write about it, the feelings go from my brain through the pencil to the paper and I feel better.

Learning about yourself can be a painful experience, but the payoff is worth it. I remember one point in my life when I realized that the one constant in all the unhappy relationships I had ever been involved in, was me. That was pretty depressing until I noticed what a good deal that was. If the problem was the other people, there was nothing I could do about it. But hey, if it was only me, I could change that!!

Okay, the newest section of your notebook can be called "My Business" or You might even name it - "Miranda Smith, Inc." Mark the following as important things to consider:

- ✓   perception of self
- ✓   assets and liabilities
- ✓   specialness
- ✓   mentors and role models
- ✓   analyzing the marketplace
- ✓   ongoing process.

So, here's the formula: $SG+S+SK=W$. Or for the less symbol oriented, specific goals plus schedule plus self-knowledge equals work. You're finally ready to pursue work.

The reason people have such a hard time conceiving how to translate their acting skills into gainful employment is that there is so much involved in the process and, like riding a bicycle, until you get the hang of it, the whole ordeal can be somewhat paralyzing. You'll have to learn to function as

- ○ a producer
- ○ a director
- ○ a detective
- ○ a press agent
- ○ a gambler
- ○ a graduate student
- ○ a psychologist
- ○ a philosopher
- ○ an entrepreneur

but don't be dismayed, after a little practice, these dormant skills will become second nature.

Looking For Work

The best way to look for work is to work. Impossible, right? You can't be in the union until you get a job, but you can't have a job until you are in the union.

That's not exactly true, you just can't find *union* work. I know you want to join the union and become a 'professional' actor as soon as possible, but have patience, it's not wise to join the union until you have amassed a few impressive credits and in LA/NY at least, have some film to show. At that point, when you are actually marketable, *then* it's time to join the union.

In the meantime, read the newspaper. See what's happening. If a theater group is casting, go there. Try out for something. Find out the name of the play, buy a copy and read it. If you are right for a part, select the scene that shows that character best and learn it. Get a friend to read it with you and be prepared to read that scene when you arrive.

If management wants you to do a different scene, don't be afraid to suggest the one you are familiar with. They will probably let you do it. If not, ask for 20 minutes to work on the alternate scene before reading. *Do not* read cold. You will never do as well as if you had prepared the material. No matter how well you think you are able to 'cold read,' it will never be the work you could do if you were able to prepare ahead of time.

If you sing, offer your services at church or at a Lions Club Dinner. Wherever something is happening, become a part of it. Be the master of ceremonies at the charity auction or be the host who greets everybody. Take every opportunity to get up in front of people, no matter how menial and you'll find that with experience comes heightened self esteem as well as skill. People will begin to think of you as *the* person who helps make their event work. If nothing is happening, find a way to stimulate some activity. If you get tired of being the one who always starts the merry-go-round, you are in the wrong business.

Whether you are in Podunk, New York or Los Angeles, you have to make your own opportunities.

Getting and Taking a Meeting

It's preferable to send a note to a potential employer that precedes a picture and resume. Pictures and resumes may sit in a pile by the door waiting until it's 'look at the pictures and resumes' day. Letters are opened immediately. Particularly those that are on *good* paper and are typed.

Last year I met a lovely young actress. I saw her work a time or two and thought she showed some promise. One day she showed me the letter she was sending out to casting directors. I knew immediately one of the reasons she was not getting their attention.

The paper looked like the cheapest dime store note paper and her handwriting looked like someone in primary school. While it is not a sin to have sub-standard handwriting and cheap paper, it does not demand you be taken seriously. Do without something else and invest in good paper and a typewriter or go to a copy center and pay to have the letter typed.

When you actually do get someone's attention and have a meeting (as opposed to an audition - and frequently in order to *get* an audition) there are several things you can do whether or not you have a resume and/or are scared witless.

Make sure your shoes are polished. Your clothes don't have to be expensive, but they should be clean, well pressed and in good repair. The care you take with your person projects the care you take in general.

Make sure your handshake is strong and that you have something to talk about. If there's a bowling trophy on a table, mention that your father bowled or whatever. Don't lie, but find an authentic way to connect with the other person.

Sit back in the chair, don't slump. They may be buying an actor who is going to play a bum, but they want to know that the actor is strong, has his own ideas and is unafraid.

Employers are putting a property in an actor's hands. It is a huge responsibility and demands a great deal of energy. If you are playing the leading role and you are frightened and don't have a vision of how to do it, they do not want to know that. This is as true for an executive at IBM as it is for an actor.

After the meeting and/or audition, sit down and make a list of all the things you did well and all the things you could have done better. Review this material before the next meeting. It will pay off.

Get Used to It

The bad news is that this constant selling is *never* over. You may as well face the facts now as later. Your whole career is going to be spent making people think they *must* employ you. Yes, there will be those times when you are semi-regularly employed, but the bottom line is that you are a self-employed person. You are responsible for keeping the momentum going once you get it started.

Careers go through moments of heat when they appear to sustain themselves, but don't lose your fire-starting skills, for as night follows day, cold follows heat and you'll be in the 'momentum starting business' again.

Taking Care of Business

Keep a Rolodex of business contacts. In New York and Los Angeles, this might mean casting directors, producers, directors, agents, etc. In a smaller town, it might mean ad agencies, radio personnel, newspaper people; whoever buys talent in your marketplace.

Note every contact; when you met, spoke and/or wrote, what the contact was about, results, etc. Record the person's physical description and where he sits in the office so you will be sure to recognize him next time. Note something the two of you talked about as well as any personal information you might have on him.

Go through your Rolodex at least once a week to see who you need to call or write a note to. Keep in touch even if there isn't something specific to talk about. Remember those AT&T commercials: You never know what will come out of a phone call.

It's not easy to do all these things. It takes energy and sometimes it's scary. Even though it may appear fruitless, it isn't. All the energy you put out will come back, maybe not today or tomorrow, but it all comes back. Practice using your imagination, creativity and courage every day and it will get easier, after all, these people are your business partners.

Respond to Good Work

Everybody likes to know their work has been recognized. Call or write a note to a casting director that you have worked with and tell her what a good job she did on a specific project. Directors and producers you have worked with will also appreciate recognition. Anne Archer tells a wonderful story about working with Glenn Close. As the star of their film, "Fatal Attraction," Glenn saw the first roughcut. She immediately sat down and wrote a detailed letter to Anne citing her best moments, scene by scene. Could you ever forget that kind of generosity?

When I was in Spain filming "A Touch of Class" and still very new to the cast, we were all sitting in a big old hotel dining room which had been converted into a screening room to show us dailies. It was uncomfortable and close, but in the middle of the screening, someone crawled all the way across the dark room, through a tangle of chairs and legs and tapped me on the knee. It was George Segal telling me he thought my work was good. I'll never forget how that made me feel.

Scratching Isn't All Bad

You aren't going to believe me, but I have to say it anyway: *early success can be the kiss of death.* With success comes visibility and judgement. Everyone waits to see if you are a "flash in the pan" and can live up to your early promise. You no longer have the luxury of anonymity in which to refine your art; therefore, it's much more expensive and scary to change anything. What if no one likes your work when you change directions? So now not only are you afraid to experiment, but you may get an unrealistic picture of the business. Seem unlikely? Let's assume you get to Los Angeles and because you are cute and adorable and young and *new*, you luck into a large or small part on a television series. Whether it runs two years or ten, the following things have happened: You've made more money than ever before and probably adjusted your lifestyle accordingly. You are recognizable or semi-recognizable (depending on the status of the show). Production assistants call you 'Miss' or 'Mr.' and get chairs and food for you. Producers and directors treat you with great respect and listen intently to your ideas and complaints (whether or not they act on them).

Regardless of the tenure of the show, you have had *one* job and played *one* part. Unless you scored a T.V. movie during your hiatus (and only really visible players on top ten rated shows usually have that option) or scored a play during that same time span, you have not grown as an actor at all. But while you were regularly employed, you never noticed and no one seemed to care. What a surprise when the show is over and you now have to fetch your own coffee and no one wants to know you. You are now considered 'over exposed' and have to sit out a few years on television while the public stops identifying you as that character.

Hector Elizondo spoke of other dangers as well:

• *The danger, of course, is in insulating yourself, especially if you become popular. You lose sight of the rest of the world. Luckily all this commercial attention has happened at this time of my life, because I've seen what it does to folks who are not ready for it at a very early age. And it's devastating because you have a tendency to slip into the illusory world of believing that you are important, and believing that what you are doing is valuable and terrific.*

The biggest danger is compromising your standards of work. Because everyone is patting you on the back, you lose sight of your limitations, your objectives, your growth - - suddenly showing up is enough.

The problem is that if you're too young and it

happens too soon, you get buried under the illusion of it.

"From "Pretty Woman" to Plenty Busy -
Elias Stimac
Drama-Logue
Sept. 19-26, 1991

Process Process Process

As long as you don't start taking yourself too seriously (whether you are currently working or out of work), you will be fine. It is imperative that you are able to conceptualize the ups and downs as 'part of the process'. A job is just a job, some are more visible, some are more lucrative, and though you may be able to figure out a way to capitalize on it, the job *will* be still over. Make sure you have a life to return to when you're no longer in fashion.

Michael Douglas was a success on a television series called "The Streets of San Francisco." Many actors might have banked that money, considered themselves a success and waited out the overexposure and lack of work that frequently comes after such high visibility and hoped for the best. But Michael wanted a film career and when no one appeared to be interested, Michael, being the entrepreneurial person that he is, figured out a way to become a real force in the business: fourteen years earlier, his father had bought the rights to a property in which he hoped to star. Michael rescued the orphaned material and found a way to make "One Flew Over the Cuckoo's Nest" a successful Academy Award-winning film. As a successful producer, Michael had the attention of the film community, but still no one came forward with interesting acting offers, so Michael produced and starred in the huge hit, "Romancing the Stone." Now, of course, he does not have to produce his own projects in order to be offered meaty parts.

It's true he had a rich, powerful and successful father and because of his background, he must have had some inkling of how business was conducted in the film community. It's also true that not all star off-spring manage to translate this largesse into brilliant careers. The bottom line is that Michael Douglas went in and created his own professional life.

In the old studio days, it was possible to be discovered. Potential was recognized, signed, and groomed for stardom. Today actors who want to work must recognize their own potential, nurture it, watch it blossom and learn to sell it themselves.

Don't Rush

After you learn to be pushy, learn to be patient. In the beginning, you are not going to work for two or three years, maybe more. Prepare for that. It's part of the process. It takes a long time not only to tune your instrument and perfect your craft, but to work your way into the system.

When people talk about networking, they don't really mean you should try to become friends with Jeff Sagansky (the president of CBS); they mean you should be a real friend to your peers. These are the stars, producers, writers and directors of tomorrow. They will rise to the top in the same time frame as you and you all can help each other. You know and trust each other. There is nothing sweeter than working with your friends.

Go Out There and Get Your Fifty Nos

There seems to be a certain no to yes ratio. Some actors say they get ten nos to every yes they receive. There are some periods of one's career when it certainly seems like you need fifty nos to get a yes. It's part of the business. That being the case, you may as well get started. The only problem is, every time you get a yes, there will still be fifty more nos lined up there someplace in your career waiting for you.

My brother is a salesman who seemingly thrives on abuse. Whenever a prospective customer keeps him waiting or treats him rudely, Jim just smiles to himself. He believes that people basically do feel guilty about bad behavior and he makes sure he capitalizes on that guilt by getting an even bigger order.

Whether you live in Dallas, Des Moines, New York or LA, the issues are the same:

- *Who in the marketplace employs actors?*
- *How can I become employed?*
- *What jobs other than straight acting are especially suitable to actors?*

If you are in New York or Los Angeles, it is easy to figure out that the major areas of employment are theater, film, television and commercials. Yet even there, the life of an actor is not all Macbeth and Bayer aspirin commercials. As a matter of fact, *most* of it isn't.

In those primary entertainment centers, actors work in industrial shows, are spokespersons for conventions and do voice overs for radio and television commercials. They supply American dialogue for foreign films, appear in front of Madison Square Garden wearing sandwich boards and handing out buttons. They lie on mattresses in department store windows and do weird commercials on "Saturday Night Live." They spend a lot of money sending out pictures and resumes and spend hours waiting on line for 'open calls' for parts that have probably already been cast. Not only that, most of them feel grateful for any opportunity to get up in public to perform, to add to their resume and mostly *make money* in anything related to the business.

If there are no opportunities for straight acting in plays, etc., isolate the kind of situation that will give you a chance to make a living within the atmosphere of 'show business.' Perhaps you can be the film critic on local radio or put together a cooking show on T.V.

Years ago, when I was in the smaller marketplace of Dallas, one of the important jobs for local actors was the annual Automobile Show in conjunction with the State Fair of Texas. If you were pretty/handsome enough, you might be employed to stand by the car all day in evening attire looking for all the world like a very expensive accessory. If you were p/h and could also *talk*, you might be the spokesperson who would speak while p/h pointed to the various features of the car.

You can do anything if you have nerve. One summer after the regular season was over at the Margo Jones Theater, where I was lucky enough to apprentice, I wondered:

• *What is it like to go into an agent's office in Dallas, Texas?*

This was in 1955 and Dallas was not the entertainment center it is has become. I looked in the phone book and found that, indeed, Dallas did have an agency. It was called The Molly O'Day Agency. I appeared and announced that I was a singer. Coached by Betty Grable movies, I was expecting to be shown the door.

• *Do you have an accompanist?*

Negative. Again, I expected the door.

• *Do you have any music?*

No, again.

• *Wait here.*

Miss O'Day went down the hall and reappeared with an accordion player. Well, I *had* sung twice in the variety show in college and I did know my key for a couple of songs. After a couple of choruses of "I'm Looking Over a Four Leaf Clover" and "It Had to be You," the accordion player left and I was offered a job singing at a nearby Air Force base in the officer's club. My natural chutzbah got me that far, but my Catholic school training prevailed and I was unable to actually look at my audience, so my Air Force singing career was pretty short.

I also worked conventions. For one of them, I was dressed as a woman from space who did a voice-less skit. The audience had to pick up earphones to hear what we were mouthing, but they could never figure how our mouths matched what was coming out of the earphones. They didn't know we had little earphones under the space caps. This job entailed being able to move well, learning dialogue and lip syncing.

I had a lucrative recurring job with Polaroid requiring that I pose with and take pictures of all the guests at a particular trade show. They trained me to set up the lights for the camera, take test pictures and deal with all the equipment AND all the guests.

I taught acting at my high school alma mater, started a children's theater and wrote my own material. I used a community room at a bank for the children's classes and aligned myself with the merchants in a shopping center. On holidays, I produced short plays in keeping with the occasion and the shopping center provided space, prizes or handouts and publicity for the event. My students had the chance to perform for more than their parents and friends. The event was successful for both merchants and students and I was making my first money in show business. It was not an extravagant amount of money, but when you start any business, you have to be prepared for meager earnings the first few years.

An actress friend started in an even smaller market: Alice, Texas. She found a way to make money from her theater degree by making book reviews her specialty. Rosemary read the latest best seller, condensed the story and then contacted the ladies' clubs and service organizations and offered her services. Clubs of this type are always looking for luncheon activities. She would tailor her review to the event, tell a couple of jokes and charge $50 or whatever the traffic would bear.

As in all other phases of this business, work begets work. She did a good job and other calls started coming in soon. She became the star of her town. It wasn't enough to keep her in caviar, but a little here and a little there all add up.

When I met her, she had moved to Dallas and was intimidated by what seemed to her to be a really big city. Since I was beginning what turned out to be six years of pregnancy, I willed her all my old jobs. She was smart and parlayed them into even more.

When the Tatum O'Neill film, "Paper Moon," filmed in Dallas, Rosemary got a part. Besides acting whenever she gets a chance, I was not surprised to discover she now writes a column for a local newspaper.

If you live in a small town, you might have to go to a neighboring town to find work. When I moved to Norman, Oklahoma, the first thing I did was look up advertising agencies in the yellow pages in Oklahoma City, which was 30 minutes away. I checked to see if they produced television commercials and asked whom I could see. By that time I had done commercials in Dallas, and those credits helped. My husband was a graduate student at the University of Oklahoma right in Norman, so I called up the motion picture department and ended up doing a few educational films for them. Money for me and film for my future.

Every working actor has a pocketful of similar stories. Successful actors call and ask where the jobs are. You need to have the imagination and determination to call *everybody*.

Unemployed/Not Working

There is a real difference between being an *unemployed* actor and *not working*. 'Not working' implies that you usually do. But once identified as unemployed, casting directors don't really want to know you. What a casting director wants, more than anything, is to think he has discovered a terrific actor with impressive credits that no one knows anything about. He can now come up with a 'fresh face' who is somehow experienced without being overexposed and doesn't have a big price tag. Buying talent is just like buying a dress, everybody loves to think he's getting a bargain.

Getting Noticed

Actors have been using their creativity for centuries figuring out how to get people to notice them. Post card campaigns. Balloon deliveries. Presents. Candy. Strip-O-Grams. These ideas have been used on agents so many times that they engender little more than a smile or a shake of the head coupled with eyes rolled heavenward.

I know an actor who did something *extremely clever*, only to have his agent (who had supported his idea initially) turn on him when the casting directors became offended.

The actor spent a lot of money, time and imagination creating a milk carton filled with candy which he had delivered to the casting directors. The gimmick was that his picture was on all the milk cartons. Under it was written the word *missing*. The actor had been out of work for some length of time and was looking for a way to get himself back before the buyers. The milk carton also listed his description, credits and agent's phone number.

As it turned out, some of the casting directors became offended with the milk carton idea. They felt that the whole idea of missing children and milk cartons was too important to be joked about. Well, of course, they're right. The actor had been so caught up in his own cleverness, he had not taken in the whole picture.

Call yourself to the casting director's attention without seeming desperate and/or unemployed. Actors wring their hands and say:

How?

By doing good work. If you have to produce it yourself, do it. If you are good, the material is 'right' and you are ready, agents and casting directors will find you. In the meantime, you are your own agent. Look at all casting notices. Be in plays. Get up in front of people at every opportunity. This is part of your training and part of your life. People don't become actors to be shrinking violets.

The other part of this equation (that I cannot stress too strongly) is that one must get out of the business of 'being chosen' and into the business of 'acting'. That means that it may be even more valuable to mount your own vehicle and act in it than for somebody else to hire you.

Gretchen Cryer and Nancy Ford, writer and composer of "I'm Getting My Act Together and Taking It on the Road," say they only began being taken seriously when they began to produce their own material. Earlier productions had been noticed, but when they 'put their money on the table', they became members of the 'fraternity.'

I know how easy it is to be caught up in the madness of *I am only valid if somebody else chooses me*, but if you indulge that kind of thinking, your life will be a nightmare. If you are constantly focused on getting someone to choose you, you can never become a valid person because you will always be second guessing what someone else might want. Do they want me to be funny here? uglier? prettier? They don't *know*. When you go shopping you don't always know exactly what you want, but your eye catches something and you *know:*

Yes, this is what I want, I didn't even know it existed, but I must have it.

Casting Directors

Most beginning (and even experienced actors) wouldn't dream of trying to call on a casting director personally, but casting directors are not as inaccessible as your fantasies might lead you to believe. I have a friend who had been quite successful as an actor in commercials in New York. For some reason (he now doesn't know why either), he had the idea that when he moved to Los Angeles, agents would be waiting for him with open arms. Of course, anyone who has spent any time in Los Angeles (or New York) will be happy to tell you that being a commercial actor or even a soap actor doesn't mean much to film and television people. It is a whole different part of the business.

My friend, a very business-oriented and determined type, decided to do for himself what agents would not. He would get himself in to see the casting directors. He made a list and every day he targeted five c.d.'s to call. He sent a picture and resume and when he made the follow-up call, he always found out with whom he was speaking and noted the name and date in his Rolodex.

Invariably, the c.d. (or assistant) would say he

was not seeing anyone right now. My friend would ask when he would be seeing people again. If the c.d. said three weeks, the actor would write that date down on his card and call in three weeks. This would go on until he actually got an appointment.

His feeling was that people begin to feel guilty after a while, and will finally see you just because they can't handle saying 'no' again. He got a lot of jobs that way and eventually landed an agent.

So, if a casting director tells you to call back in three weeks, call in three weeks. Always call the person by name:

• *Hi, Mary? This is Kelly Smith again. How are you? What did you think about the Academy Awards* (Dodgers, earthquake, etc.)? *Well, here I am again. Just wondering if you have any time for me to come meet with you. I'm going to be over in that direction tomorrow anyway.*

Elizabeth Pena, who starred in "Batteries Not Included," "La Bamba" and "Jacob's Ladder," got her first job in a feature in a similar way.

After several fruitless months in Los Angeles, she read of the then upcoming feature "Down and Out In Beverly Hills" directed by Paul Mazursky, who liked Latins. Undeterred by the fact that she had no agent, Pena began bombarding the film's casting director with photos, letters and resumes. She finally persuaded a studio guard to deliver a demo tape and eventually wound up with the role of the sultry maid, Carmen:

• *I believe you should just go for it. There's no door thick enough; if it's too thick, you blast it open. If you*

have to get through, you have to get through.
"Close Ups" -
Libby Slate
American Premier
The Magazine of the Film Industry
Spring 1988

Kathy Najimy, who played the perennially bubbly
smiling nun in "Sister Act" is another proponent of
taking things into her own hands.   A real power-
house, Kathy had already spent time doing stand-up,
improvisation and political theater when:

• *She teamed up with another entrepreneur, Mo
Gaffney to form their feminist cabaret act, "The Kathy
and Mo Show: Parallel Lives," a collage of character
vignettes that ran for a year and a half Off-Broadway,
collected several Obies and was made into an HBO
special.*

*Spinning off from the duo, Najimy was cast in
six movies within two years.*

*Najimy and Gaffney have teamed up again, co-
writing a comedy under the guidance of Nora Ephron.
The script is part of a two picture writing deal with
Hollywood Pictures; she also has a CBS development
deal.*

*When it comes to her career as an actress and
comedian, Najimy follows a motto - from Nike: "Just
do it." 'I just try to go out and get things,' she says.*
"The Wit Under the Wimple" -
Randee Mia Berman
The Los Angeles Times
June 2, 1992

Action breeds success; go get things, go make things

happen, go do the work.

Once you become a 'force' financially, there will be agents and managers who will want to hitch their wagons to yours and may even initiate work for you, but your vision still needs to fuel the engine.

An Agent Is Not Necessarily the Answer

On any given day, in any given city, where there are theatrical agents, you'll find disgruntled actors who will tell you their agents never get them any work at all. And they may be right.

I believe that the best agent in the world can't sell you if you are not a marketable product. It's still up to you to create that product and to keep making it marketable. One of the ways to do that is with publicity.

Self-Promotion

It's amazing how much publicity you can actually get for yourself. One follows the same procedure in New York, Podunk or Indianapolis. Although you can just send information addressed "To the Editor," you will have better luck if you will do a little research.

Target a periodical and read it for a bit to digest a couple of names. When you are ready to submit material, call the editorial department and ask to speak to the person at the publication that your research has uncovered as most likely to be interested in your type of information. This will usually be the entertainment or theater editor, but you might be able to slant your story toward general features if you can tie in another element. In any event, make sure you ask for and send to the appropriate person *by name.*

If I were publicizing this book, I might call the entertainment editor or the books editor. If I slanted the story to include not only the information available in the book, but how I happened to write it in the first place and how this is my fourth successful book, then the story would appeal to a larger audience.

If you are appearing in a play, you can send a blurb when you are cast and later, when you are opening, send another. If anything interesting or funny happened during rehearsal, you might get a few lines recounting the incident. Send in the information, they may need a filler.

Call and attempt to speak to the writer before you send material and then follow-up to see that your information arrived. On the first call, say something like,

*Hello, Jane Smith? This is Laura Adams, I saw your piece on "Performing Pigs" and really thought it was funny. I cut it out and sent it to my mother (*chit-chat/chit-chat*). The reason I'm calling is that I'm producing a play and I have an idea about it that I thought might interest you. Since it's turned out that everyone in the cast was in the first grade together (*or whatever else you can dream up that might be unusual or interesting and make a newstory*) I thought this might make a nice feature. May I send you some information?*

She'll either say 'no' (in which case you have saved postage and can now call up another newspaper or dream up another "hook") or she'll say, 'yes.' If she does agree to your plan, verify the exact address and tell her you'll call in a couple of days to make sure she received your packet. Then make sure you do so.

I called <u>The Daily News</u>, <u>The Los Angeles Times</u> and <u>Daily Variety</u> in Los Angeles asking general questions regarding whether one needed a publicist in order to get coverage. I asked if actors were 'looked down upon' if they were calling for themselves. On the contrary, the editors informed me, they would prefer to talk directly to the actor. Perhaps more to a celebrity than you or me, but they did say they would, so put them to the test. If you have something truly newsworthy or funny, they will be thrilled to have it.

If you are trying to get material in a special column, call the columnist, introduce yourself and ask if he accepts material directly from actors. If he does, ask if you might send something. Drop it by personally if possible. If you don't get to see him, follow up with a phone call to make sure he got the material and thank him for his help. Be careful with his time, but take the time to be personal.

Following up takes more time and energy, but you get out what you put in. If you take the easiest route, your rewards will invariably not be as great.

In all cases, *take the time* to make a professional-looking presentation of your material *and* slant the material in a unique manner. Make sure the story is typed and double-spaced and include a contact name, address, phone number. In a small town, it's a little simpler to get space and maybe, a picture. Television and radio are not that difficult, if you can think of an angle. The media has space and time to fill every day, so if you can make your project visually interesting and unique, you'll not only meet with success, but they'll soon be happy to her from you. If you are just appearing in a play, that is probably not newsworthy, but if the play deals with some relevant topic or if you researched it in an interesting way, people will find it entertaining.

If you are directing or producing a play, you might consider dedicating the proceeds from one performance to a local charity. That way you and the charity both benefit from the publicity. Arrange a contest within the theme of the play. Have a look-a-like contest. There are all sorts of ways to get the media interested, particularly in a small town. Try imagining each program you are contacting as if it were your own. If you were the host of that show, what would appeal to you? Various radio stations in Los Angeles give away free tickets to plays providing important 'plugs'. Become aware of what's going on in the media in your area and some way of fitting in will occur to you.

Fans

No matter where you live, you will begin to collect some fans along the way. Don't discount them. Fans are a symbol of your growing visibility. When I was still in high school, it meant so much to me when actors personally answered my letters giving me advice that I always respond to fans who write asking for guidance and send pictures when people request them.

Many actors have a mailing list and send out postcards to fans when they are going to appear in something. If you can get someone interested enough to be your fan club president, they can do those things for you. If you are ever involved in an endeavor that needs support from the public to prove to your employer it is important to keep hiring you, your fans are there to take on the challenge. That's how "Cagney &

Lacey," "Designing Women," "Home Front" and innumerable other television shows have kept themselves on the air in the past.

Pictures & Resumes

No matter what market you are in, you are going to have to come up with pictures and resumes. You will need pictures for the newspapers, casting directors and producers as well as to introduce yourself to the various organizations in your community.

Look at other actors' pictures to see what appeals to you when selecting a photographer. Look at all the other pictures that have ever been taken of you, including snapshots. Isolate what is most interesting about the best ones. If you feel you can't analyze them appropriately, consider taking a photography or art class to develop a more discerning eye.

Wardrobe

Consider the purpose of the photos when you are choosing wardrobe. Commercial casting directors usually like to see you in plain shirts/blouses and sweaters, on the other hand musical promotion requires a much more trendy approach. Study record covers for ideas. Make sure your photo fulfills the appropriate criteria.

In general, buyers are interested in a full-front representation of *you*. No hands up to the face; it's too distracting. Choose clothing that is relatively plain. You're not selling clothes, you want them looking at you. Unless you are shooting color, black and white clothing is usually not a good choice because the severe contrast is not flattering. Red, green and other medium tones usually photograph more appealingly.

The most important aspect of any photo is that it look *exactly* like you. It's self-defeating to choose a photographer who takes glamour photos if you are a regular person. If a casting director calls you in expecting to see Jaclyn Smith and you are Rhea Perlman, he is not going to be pleased. Forget about trying to change people's minds, casting directors are busy. They have their orders from on high and they are trying to fill them. Later they will be needing Rhea Perlman.

Analyze every picture you see. Look at the pictures your friends are using, but don't let those pictures make your decisions, just use them for research. Make up your own mind. When I am choosing my own pictures from a contact sheet, I try to decide which of the images is the person I would want to approach and speak to at a party.

If you have an agent, it is always wise to get his input regarding these decisions since he will be selling you via the pictures. He will have concrete ideas about what is best. Learn more by asking him how he made his choices.

It's usually not a good idea to let photographers choose. Their criteria for a good picture involves lighting and composition. They are not necessarily in a position to know what is the best representation of you relative to selling yourself as an actor.

An 8x10 glossy print is sent with your resume. You can have your picture printed with or without a white border (some agents prefer the picture without border, but it is usually more expensive). The resume should be stapled to the back so that as you turn the picture over, you see the resume as though it were printed on the back side of the photo. The buyers see hundreds of resumes every day. Yours should be simple and easy to read. Not only is it not necessary to have millions of jobs listed, but when prospective employers see too much writing, their eyes will glaze over and they won't read anything. Choose the most impressive credits and list them. There is a prototype on the next page for you to use as a guide for form. You may have nothing to put on your resume, if that's true, at least list your training and a physical description. Lead with your strong suit. If you have done more commercials than anything else, list that as your first category; if you are a singer, list 'music'. You may live in a market where theater credits are taken very seriously. If this is so, even though you may have done more commercials, lead with theater if you have anything credible to report. Adapt this prototype to meet your needs. If all you have done is college theater, list it. That is more than someone else has done and it will give the buyer an idea of what you can do.

If you do book reviews, list places where you did them. If you sing, list where. Note that you were master of ceremonies for your town Pioneer Day Celebration. Whatever. As you have more important credits, drop the less impressive ones.

My own opinion is not to put your union affiliation (Screen Actors Guild, Actors Equity Association, American Federation of Television and Radio Artists) on the resume. As far I am concerned, if you list them, you are making a big deal of it. If you are a member of the unions, of course you are. If you are not that far along yet, don't bring it to their attention.

Mary Smith\555-4489
5'4", 115 lbs, Blonde hair, blue eyes

Theater

Hamlet . . . . name of theater
Lost in Yonkers . . . . name of theater

Film

Tootsie . . . . name of director
Soapdish . . . . name of director

Television

Who's the Boss? . . . . name of director
LA Law . . . . name of director

Commercials

First National Bank, Local Gas Company, Local
Newspaper, etc.

Training

acting . . . . teacher
singing . . . . teacher
dance . . . . teacher

skills: Speak Spanish fluently, horseback riding,
gymnastics, ballroom dancing, commercial
driving license, etc.

The most important thing on your resume is that your name and phone number be prominently displayed. If you have an agent, use his phone number at the bottom of the document instead of yours. If you don't have an agent, get an answering service or phone mail and use that number instead of your own. It's safer and more professional not to list your personal number for business phone calls.

Telephones

No matter what, have *call waiting*. You cannot afford for a buyer to have difficulty reaching you. Have a reliable answering service or answering machine. Some paranoid souls (me, for one) have both for that off-day when the phone is out of order.

Securing Work

People think job seeking as an actor is not exactly like looking in the *help wanted* section of your newspaper or looking in the yellow pages. Actually, the concept is not all that different.

I went to the library today and looked in the yellow pages at a cross section of phone books just to see what the possibilities of employment were. I looked up St. Paul, MN; Des Moines, IA; Phoenix, AZ and Tacoma, WA. The yellow pages of each of these cities all listed Entertainers and Entertainment Agencies. The biggest possibilities involved singers, (there were lots of musical and variety agents) comedians, magicians, etc. Some listed speakers and most listed those services having to do with conventions and fairs. Phoenix listed something called 'Ladies Choice' (your guess is as good as mine). 'The

Bag Lady' in Tacoma also aroused my curiosity.

Get in the habit of scanning the classified section of your newspaper, you'd be surprised to see that (though rare) there are some casting notices.

Once you feel ready, set goals and begin being businesslike about creating your own work, it's time to call on advertising agencies, television stations, film companies, promotional organizations, casting directors, directors and/or producers.

When you get an appointment, arrive early, look terrific and be calm. Do some deep breathing in your car before you come in order to settle your nerves. Remember your goal is for the two of you to do business together. This is less threatening than thinking you want this person to give you a job. Focus on what you have to bring to the event. If you don't have anything to contribute, perhaps you should not be there.

In Chapter Three we talked a little about recognizing the jobs that might be available in your marketplace and briefly discussed how to talk to people when you call. You might want to review that.

Here's a new chapter for your notebook: Things to remember when looking for work:

- ✓ taking care of business
- ✓ responding to good work
- ✓ patience
- ✓ process
- ✓ rejection
- ✓ perspective
- ✓ publicity
- ✓ casting directors
- ✓ relationships with fans
- ✓ pictures and resume

✓   telephone accessibility
✓   how to look for work

I hope by now that your imagination has been stimulated and you are already thinking of ways to translate this information into ideas for your hometown.

Now for the fun stuff.

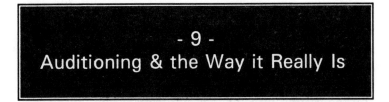

After all your hard work, you have progressed beyond trying to get someone's attention - - to having a meeting with them - - to actually being called to audition.

All auditions are different. Sometimes there will be only a casting director who will read with you, but sometimes the producers and directors are there with the c.d. In Los Angeles, there might be 20 people in the room when you arrive. At first glance, seeing all those people might rattle you, but if you take the attitude of

Oh boy! It's a bigger audience!

you'll be using the circumstances to your advantage.

In most markets, the casting director holds preliminary auditions, selects those considered most appropriate and calls these people back to be reviewed by the director and/or producer. Sometimes the preliminary audition is taped and those tapes are shown to the buyers who make decisions regarding callbacks.

Auditions can take many forms. Commercial auditions traditionally entail many, many actors who are called to (actually) read for a casting director and/or producers and/or directors, usually in a conference room.

Theatrical auditions are frequently held onstage in a theater, but are also regularly held in meeting rooms when a theater is unavailable. It might be important for you to find out before the audition just where it will be held. Your preparation might be different for a small office than a large theater.

Film and television auditions are usually held in a meeting room. If your work is not already known by the casting director, she will screen you before presenting you to the producers and/or directors.

Preparation

Prepare carefully. If you don't want the job, don't go. You won't do your best work and there is no way of erasing a bad impression from a roomful of people who just saw you do bad work. You never know who is sitting in and when they might have a job that you would be right for. People remember.

A few months ago I got a job for which I didn't audition. I scanned the list of people involved with the project, searching for a familiar name. How had I gotten this job? On the set, the director reminded me that we had worked together *seven* years ago. I had one scene on a T.V. movie that I couldn't remember. He did.

There is a wonderful book I strongly recommend, "Audition" by Michael Shurtleff. The book was so nourishing and instructive that when I first read it, I wanted to sleep with it under my pillow. His descriptions of Barbra Streisand's early auditions alone are worth the price of the book. I feel the same way about Allan Miller's new book, "A Passion for Acting" which also talks a lot about Streisand.

Each actor has his own way of attacking a project. Even if you are going to read only a few lines, it is worth *every* effort to get your hands on the script ahead of time and read the entire script at least twice before focusing on your scene.

It means everything to me to be able to read the material aloud with another human being prior to the audition. Sometimes there is no one around to do this with and I just have to take my best shot. I have been known to pay the neighborhood kids to read lines with me. I just pay their babysitting rate. Some people work with other actors and take that actor along with them to the audition.

If you are to provide your own material, choose carefully. Unless specifically asked, do not bring Shakespeare or another classic. These parts will not show your castability. No matter how well you do it, the material makes the primary impression so if you can entertain and charm them with an appealing script, your chances are better. Actors win Academy Awards every year for being lucky enough to get the role that shows them to their best advantage.

When I was a student of Herbert Berghof's at the HB Studios in New York, he used to suggest that the best material for an actor was novels and plays written by an author from the actor's own region and background. It's not that difficult to choose scenes from a novel and write phrases that bridge the dialogue if it does not stand as is. When you work with material written by an author raised with your same sensibilities, you will bring an unconscious truth that cannot be acted and when you work from a novel, you have material that is more interesting to your auditioners because of it's originality.

It's not wise to do memorable scenes associated with famous actors. You may be really fabulous, but while you are doing Robert DeNiro's role in "Taxi Driver", they are wishing Mr. DeNiro was present.

When you prepare for the audition, make sure

you are specific. Whatever is in your mind when you are doing the scene will show. If confusion and fear are your primary concerns instead of the emotion of the scene and the lines are only coming out of your mouth without access to your brain, confusion and fear will be the message they receive.

Although there is a difference of opinion about dressing for the part for an audition, I always do (within reason). I don't do it for them; I do it for me. Dressing in character helps feed my feelings for the scene. As you dress, think about how your character would go about dressing and how the character feels.

Another facet of auditioning (and acting, of course) is character. If you come in with a 'character' over and above what is written, whether it is an attitude, a walk or a way of speaking, you will stand out head and shoulders from the crowd.

The reason that so many stand up comedians get work is that most have honed a 'character' that they play in their act. Writers come in, see the act, steal the most interesting characteristics and write them into their scripts and sometimes, they take the comedian with it.

Peter Boyle had been working for many years when he captured the attention of the world in a film called "Joe." The words and basic value system of that character were written into the script, but in fact, Peter had invented a 'blue collar' character that he had been playing for years in various skits in "Second City" (a famous improvisational group in Chicago). When he got the chance to play Joe, he plugged in the 'character material' he had been working on for years.

If you haven't worked on creating characters, start now and add dimension to your work.

Auditioning and Waiting

In college, you only have to wait ten minutes for a full professor before you can 'walk'. I don't give much more time to casting directors and producers unless there are extenuating circumstances. If the c.d. comes out, explains the problem and apologizes, I am able to be good natured about it up to a point. After 15 minutes with no word from on high, I find a telephone, call my agent and have him deal with it. He may tell me to leave or he may make a phone call that results in the c.d. apologizing, getting me right in or making another appointment.

If you are a member of Screen Actors Guild, the client must pay an hourly rate if he keeps you waiting past one hour. Don't make a fuss, just jot down the names of some of the other waiting actors from the sign-in sheet, call SAG, mention the incident plus the other names (so the client won't be able to single out that you are the one who called) and you will ultimately get a check in the mail. It will be for one hour pro-rated from SAG minimum for an eight hour day.

Even if you are going to get paid, it's still hard to stay in a good humor, so don't wait so long that you get huffy. If you get huffy, you are dead in the water, so go ahead and leave. They're not going to want to hire an angry actor. If you are Tom Cruise or Julia Roberts, you can get by with throwing a tantrum, otherwise, forget about it. Explain that you have another audition and that you will be happy to come back. Be sure to address this *before* you get huffy and when you *will* still be happy to come back.

The longer you wait, the more your energy is dissipated by holding the anger down. It is a real test of my mettle for me to put aside the anger for being kept waiting and still do a good audition.

As a parent, I remember being instructed that if my child had a tantrum, it was my fault. My job, as the parent was to notice the signs preceding it and take steps to head it off. I try to be as caring a parent to myself as I was to my children. Therefore, I walk out of bad situations.

Audition Behavior

You will be judged from the moment you enter the audition office. Receptionists are sometimes quite powerful so be sure to acknowledge them. You don't have to be phony, but this is a human being here who doesn't appreciate being invisible any more than you do.

When you enter the audition room, take time to enter the atmosphere. Don't waste time, but take a moment to breathe. Notice who is there and what is going on. Have something to say.

You can talk about the World Series, the Super Bowl, the Oscars, or the weather. Don't be inane, but take a moment. You will feel more comfortable and so will they. This is also part of the audition. They have scheduled this time for you because they think you are worth looking at. *Take* the time.

Don't be afraid to move around. Set up the room as you want. Go over the scene in your mind as you physically take in the room to visualize yourself in the scene. The casting director will be happy to take the cue from you about when to begin the scene. If she begins the scene before you are ready, just say you need another moment to prepare. Turn your back, get in character, remember what went on in the script in the moment just before this scene and begin with that energy.

Insecurity

Some actors think they can take the edge off their insecurity and humanize themselves by commenting on their fears in the audition room. Trust me, insecurity is not appealing to the buyer. There is too much money at stake. No one really wants to hear about your impending nervous breakdown. They're worried about their own and they want to feel that they have found the actor that is going to solve all their problems, not present new ones.

Some actors speak of being so frightened at an audition that they didn't do their best. It's all very well and good for others to say, 'just relax,' but it's not that easy. That's one of the reasons it is so important to get up and perform at every opportunity. The more time you spend in front of people, the less you will be frightened.

The best way to give up your anxiety is to be so specific and concentrated in your work that you don't have time for anxiety to creep in. It takes enormous effort to really concentrate and take yourself out of the audition room and into the material. You can only do this by constantly exercising your muscles of concentration.

Every day take time to visualize something. Either the material you are working on or something that you want. Use your concentration to *emotionally* visit the situation. If you are visualizing a job, then picture yourself already having it and *feel* the feelings you would feel under those circumstances. Then in a pressured audition situation, those tools are ready for you to use.

Working with props is a good example of concentration taking the anxiety away. Props require authentic concentration to use appropriately; threading a needle, peeling a potato, washing a dish, or repairing a stool have to be done in reality or the task won't work. That *reality* grounds the actor into the scene.

Memorizing the Material

There are several schools of thought about memorizing the material for an audition. My own personal preference, which *many* casting directors say is a *bad idea*, is to memorize the scene. It's not difficult for me to memorize and I feel I do a much better job if I can free myself from the page. There have been times that it didn't work out, but I'm still not sorry I go for it. Frequently, I will announce that I am going to attempt a scene without the script and that if it doesn't work out I will use it. And sometimes I have had to.

If you do not have an easy time memorizing, don't go for it. A few years ago, I was conducting a seminar for The American Film Institute on "Auditioning and the Business of Show Business" and I gave audition material out on Saturday night for simulated auditions on Sunday. One of the actresses had memorized the scene for her 'audition' She failed to impress me in any way. In a later part of the session, I gave her some material that she had only a few minutes to prepare so there was no possibility of her memorizing it. When her energy was freed from trying to remember the lines, she was a completely different actress. Do what works best for you.

Casting directors tell me it's not only all right, but a very good idea to stop an audition that is going badly and begin again. Apologies are bad form, just smile and do better.

Negotiating

Although getting chosen is a big step towards a job, it doesn't necessarily mean you are going to work. The next hurtle is negotiation. Money, billing and working rules are laid down.

If you are in one of the performing unions, many details are already addressed in a standard contact. Whatever is not already spelled out must be negotiated. As a beginning actor, one usually is happy to do anything for any pittance, frequently for free. The actor should look upon the free work as graduate school.

When you are farther along in your profession, you will find that there are three plums possible in any job: billing, money and part. You will want to get at least one of them.

If the part stinks and the money is terrible but your billing is going to be better than you have gotten in the past, that might be a reason to take the job. If you are to get little money, and no billing, but the part is sensational, for heaven's sake take the job! Maybe all that appeals to you is the money. That's not all bad, either.

Let's talk a little bit about money. Currently, scale for a day working through Screen Actors Guild is $466. Weekly (film or television) $1620. Half-hour television episodes are usually shot in five days.

Past minimum is a category called *major role* performer which involves any actor who negotiates credit before the show or on a separate card or its equivalent in a crawl at the end of the show. In those cases, the player must be paid no less than daily minimum wage for a minimum of four days on a half-hour episode ($1864) or seven days on an hour episode ($3262). If you do the math, you'll see that weekly minimum gives a discount for multiple days. Until the 'major role performer' category, most actors never noticed that what used to be referred to as "top of the show" (the so-called 'top' that any show would negotiate for guest stars other than big names) was only a few dollars more than minimum for a week. Actors happily accepted "top of the show" thinking this somehow put them into an elite. The day that real working actors got on The Screen Actors Guild Board of Directors, they brought the major performer category into the next negotiation with producers. It's not a large gain, but it is something.

Clearly, there are performers who make much more than that even though the producers swear it isn't so. It is their way of price-fixing. In any event, salaries are always 'what the traffic will bear' once you graduate past minimum. If you are hot or you don't want the job, you can demand more. Nothing makes an actor more attractive to a casting director than not wanting the job. The longer you say 'no,' the higher the fee becomes.

There is a point beyond which the c.d. will not go. If you want to get your price up, judgment is everything. As in poker, you want your adversary to put as much money on the table as possible, but you don't want him to fold.

When you really need the job, of course, it's always a different story.

Series regulars (with no important credits) usually work their first half-hour series for $2500 per show. Series regulars who are visible obviously

command much more money. One of the reasons
"Dallas" finally went off the air was that Larry
Hagman and the other regulars had (after 11 years)
negotiated their salaries to such astronomical heights
that the show was just too expensive to produce.

Quotes/Money

Quotes refer to the amount of money you were paid
for your last job. If you have been paid $5000 per
week on a movie of the week or $1500 per day on a
film, these fees would be your "quotes" and you will
be expected to cite where, when and for whom you
made this money at your next negotiation. Be truthful
for casting directors *will* check. Part of their job is to
get the best talent for the least amount of money.

All these casting directors know one another
and they share information. Actors should share, also.
It would be important to you to know that John Somebody made $2000 for a day on a particular show.
When you ask for $1500 and they say, 'we never pay
that much,' you'd know they're not playing square
with you. Never divulge your sources of information,
however, or you will lose them.

If you have been working on a per day basis at
minimum, doing good work and getting good feedback
for a period of time, it might be time to start asking
for $500 a day and then $750 per day, or whatever
increments the market will bear.

If you are unsuccessful in moving your price
up, just amass some more good credits and try again.
It will happen.

A friend of mine determined that he would no
longer work for 'major role' (a.k.a. 'top of the
show') money. Although not a star, my friend works

a lot, has a very special quality and felt he 'deserved' more. In fact, he has been able to demand 'double top' a couple of times, but the number of times per year that he has worked has dropped dramatically. You may have to decide whether you want to work more often or get paid more, particularly today:

• *Top Stops: Casting directors are telling agents, 'Get me the best actors for the least money. Don't submit anyone who won't work for scale plus ten percent.' As a result, mid-priced actors have seen salaries drop as much as 50 percent, with no room for negotiation. Top-of-the-show pay for TV guest performers is lower now than it was 10 years ago, and more name actors are competing for ever fewer guest spots. Series regulars have taken pay freezes and even cuts in order to keep their jobs. Disney just announced that the studio will not pay more than $25,000 per episode to series stars.*

> "Bad News" -
> Compiled by Mark Locher
> Screen Actor
> Spring, 1992, Volume 31, No. 1

You might be offered the part of your dreams, but the money is terrible. You have painstakingly gotten your price up to find you are now offered the perfect part for very little money. By all means, take the part. You will probably be able to get the casting director to offer you a 'no quote.' This is exactly what it says. If another c.d. tries to obtain information regarding your pay on that job, the information is unavailable. It seems to me, however, that if you have a 'no quote' the casting director must assume that you worked for less than your usual fee.

Getting Replaced

Getting the job and beginning rehearsal is no guarantee you will actually work the job although if it is a union job, you will be paid.

When I was starring on a series called "Joe's World" for NBC, I began to realize how lucky I had been in my career. We would frequently meet for the first day of rehearsal, read around the table with the guest cast and by the time we got back from lunch, we might be missing two guest cast members. Management somehow didn't think they were funny enough at the first reading. The moral here is to always put your best foot forward. There is too much money at stake for faith. You must always be showing people what you can do.

It's also not uncommon to land a pilot, work the show and be replaced when the show comes to series. Sometimes it is because the actor they originally wanted has become available. Sometimes their fantasies did not turn out to be the same as your reality. It's childish to take it as a sign that you are untalented and will surely never work again. Just examine the situation and see if there is something you might have done differently with either the people or the material. Learn and get on with it; it's self indulgent and mean to beat yourself up.

Working With Stars

Actors are just like civilians, they love famous people and feel (rightly) that working with a famous person will give them more prestige. It certainly enhances a resume. Working with stars can be just as delightful (or not) as working with everyday people.

Stars frequently direct you. It never bothers me although it makes some other actors crazy. When I feel the idea is good, I use it. On occasion I have seen stars blatantly give an actor notes that will make his performance worse, so be sure to evaluate the advice before you take it. It does no good to resist, to go to the director or to get cranky about it. Just tell the star what a great idea it is, thank him profusely and do what you want.

I once worked with a well-known actress who must have been upset that the writers had given me a very powerful scene to play. The scene called for tears. As we started to shoot my scene, the actress managed to drop something, flub a line or otherwise ruin the scene over and over.

She assumed the more we did the scene, the less emotional juice I would have to expend. Too bad for her, that day, I could do no wrong. The only thing she accomplished was to cost the producers more money because we had to shoot it so many times.

Some actors (stars or not) will purposely ruin a take if they do not like the way they looked in it. This keeps the director from making the decision to use the scene for someone else's good performance. There's not much you can do about that.

If you are working with a very competitive actor who feels he can only look good if you look bad, your only real defense is not to get hooked into it. I have heard stories of actors one-upping one another in this regard. Some actors are able to be quite powerful in offsetting this and consider it a testing of sorts and don't get all cranky about it. It can be disconcerting, but if you rise to the occasion, it can also be invigorating.

There are many stories about Marilyn Monroe

and the filming of "Some Like it Hot." She would supposedly not come out of her trailer until the afternoon. By that time, her co-stars had been waiting for her since morning. They were tired, frustrated, angry and no longer at their best.

Who knows if her tardiness was fear regarding her own performance or competition with her fellow actors?

And you don't even have to be a 'big star' to be a jerk. My friend, Leslie, told me about an experience she had shooting a T.V. movie in a small town in Pennsylvania. Much time had been spent rehearsing in New York before the company went on location so that when the day came to actually shoot, all the actors had to do was "mark" it for the camera one time and then shoot. Leslie's scene involved a verbal fight with a much more experienced actress. Leslie had all the lines while her opponent was to attempt to speak. As the director called "action" and the rehearsal began, the other actress slugged Leslie full in the face. The slap was an incredible stimulus for the scene and it played better than it had ever played. The only problem was that the camera was not rolling. Because no one had called 'cut', Leslie continued her performance at a high pitch and had nothing left when the camera *was* rolling. Whatever the motivation of the other actress, Leslie missed her own biggest moment in the film.

Protocol

Afraid of doing the wrong thing when I first worked on a set in Los Angeles, I would quietly go to my chair and sit until someone decided to speak to me. As it turned out, I now realize, this is the most appropriate way to behave.

On a film or television set, there is an unspoken hierarchy or pecking order. By and large, an extra does not go up to a star or director and begin a conversation. Neither does a supporting player, unless there is already a relationship. The star and director can approach anyone they choose. Others best wait to be recognized. It's very subtle, but very real.

There's nothing wrong with this. It's etiquette in the business. Just be cool and observe. You will understand quickly. I don't imagine a lowly secretary goes up to the President of IBM and starts a conversation either. When you become the star, it will be up to you to make others feel at home on the set.

Getting Hired

This is not a business of absolutes. As I've said before, there is luck involved. Part of playing this particular poker game is training yourself as consistently and thoroughly as possible. Study acting, singing, dancing, dialects, and fencing. The more things you are trained to do, the more parts you can be considered for.

Training and ability is a given once you are recognized as part of the talent pool. You and your competitors are all good at your work and the decision will be made on a variety of things.

'Right' for the Part

When a casting director speaks of an actor as 'right' for a part, he is speaking about the essence of the actor. We all associate a particular essence with Paul

Newman and a different essence with Woody Allen, so one would not expect that Woody Allen and Paul Newman would be up for the same part.

Another aspect of being 'right' concerns visibility. Visibility means currently being on view in film, theater or television. In this business, it is 'out of sight, out of mind.' You can be a dead ringer for Tom Cruise, but if you are not as visible as he is, you're not going to get seen for his part. The bigger the part, the bigger the credits you must to have to support being seen.

The third element of 'right' has to do with physicality. If you are 6'7" and everyone else in the project is 5'4," it does seem unlikely you will be hired. If they are putting together a family, it is necessary that you look more like the rest of the family than your closest competitor, all other things being equal.

Factors Involved in Staying Hired

People commonly think of professional behavior as being on time, learning your lines, not eating garlic and using deodorant. No one ever tells you the following:

Don't keep people waiting. If you are on a set, and the director or stage manager calls for you, *don't* finish the joke or story you are telling. Explain to whoever that you will finish later. It *is* a temptation to entertain such a captive audience, particularly if you know the latest gossip, funniest joke, etc. But three minutes here and five minutes there do add up. If you are on a film or television set, you could be holding up an enormous group of people. Not only is it expensive, it is terribly arrogant to consider that your joke (which only five people are going to hear, anyway) is important enough to keep 150 people waiting.

Don't clown around. Before entering college, I had no prior experience as an actress except for school plays at a very minor level. When I got to college, it seemed like heaven. I really wanted to be liked and chose to become a real clown at rehearsals. One day, as I was delaying rehearsals doing some funny thing, not saying the line properly to get a laugh, or whatever, I looked across the stage to my friend, Jerry Melton. Jerry was older and a much more experienced actor than I and I really looked up to him. As I looked at him, he made this face that said:

No, no. Don't do that. It's not cool.

I got it immediately and stopped. No one had ever told me and I was young and dumb. I found out later that I had not been cast in a couple of plays because I was known as someone who wasted time.

Stay off the telephone. Stay tuned in.
Recently, I guested on a television show that had a lot of young actors as leads. They varied in ages from 6 to 21. The show was not doing well for a variety of reasons, but it was woefully behind schedule because every time the cameras were ready to roll, one or another of the young stars was on the phone. It took time to get them off the phone and back to the set.

Others who might have been more conscientious and stayed close to the set saw no future in that since the set-ups were always delayed, so they started straggling about and had to be rounded up as well. Yes, it is up to the Assistant Directors and Stage Managers to make sure the actors are in their places when the camera is ready to roll, but it isn't their job to give actors lessons in manners. It's unlikely that anyone is ever going to take the time to explain to an actor:

- *You are wasting everyone's time.*
- *Your energies are focused on phone calls instead of the work at hand.*
- *Because of these things, no one will be motivated to request you on future projects.*

I was able to see myself in these actors and thought of the times that I had rushed to the phone between shots instead of staying tuned to the set and wondered not only how many people I might have alienated by this behavior, but how my work might have been affected as well.

I have a friend who is on a Top 10 television show. She has very little to do each week. She spends lots of time in her dressing room while the rest of the cast is rehearsing without her. She might have three hours off in the afternoon.

But she never rushes out to shop or takes long lunches. She doesn't spend all the time in her dressing room on her script, but she tells me that if she were to leave the studio, she would not be focused on her work. She needs to be there.

I think of another actress I know on a highly-regarded show. She doesn't have much to do, either. The difference is this: she is so angry because she feels under-utilized that she doesn't ever prepare well. Sometimes, not at all. It's only a few lines. Who needs to work on it? The result is the writers perceive this and have no incentive to write for her. She doesn't do what she is given very well, so why give her more?

Wherever you are, if you are not part of the solution, you are part of the problem.

Whatever capacity you are working in, the employer wants to know you care and that you want the whole endeavor to be the best possible product. I am never happy to pay someone to do the minimum, but it's a pleasure to pay someone money I feel they have earned and it's to my advantage to reward them with more work.

Networking

Networking is a dirty word to many of you, I know;

Oh, I'm not good at all that bullshit, etc. etc.

I don't want to get a job just because I know someone.

I'm here for art, not for commercialism, etc., etc., etc.

Come on, wouldn't *you* really rather work someplace where you feel comfortable and with a director that you already know you can trust? Well, management feels the same way and it's their money that's on the line.

That being the case, keep up with directors, producers, writers and casting people you have worked with. And that doesn't mean just sending them a note when you are appearing in something, keep up with their careers and let them know when they do something you like. They know you're an actor and that you want a job, and if you're good, hiring you will only make them look good. So do *all* of your part, keep in touch and keep growing. Besides, when you become a star, you'll want to recommend directors as well as make-up people, costumers and the best of everyone you know and admire.

Many jobs in episodes are given to people who have worked with the director before - except for smaller roles, so do as much as you can to stay connected.

Keep meticulous notes. If you meet with a casting director and are able to find out that she has a 10-year-old daughter named Diane, then that information should go on a card to help you remember the casting director and to give you something to talk about. Not only will the casting director appreciate your effort, but you will able to audition better for you will feel more comfortable. Life is about connecting, being in the moment, and treating peoples with respect. If you don't take the time to do that, it doesn't matter how many jobs you get, you'll continually feel that something is missing.

Practice connecting ALL the time. Talk to the people in the grocery store or the people at the bank. Have conversations with everybody. Practice remembering and using their names. Find out something about them. Notice what makes one person different from another. Become a student of human nature. You'll not only become a better actor, but a more appealing person as well. The act of networking will simply be keeping up with your friends.

My son is in graduate school studying Artificial Intelligence (computer stuff). When a Math star speaks on campus, his major professor makes sure his graduate students meet for coffee afterwards with the star and converse, he brings Dr. Smart to my son and says,

• *Dr. Smart, I want you to meet Jamie Callan, he is working on thus and such. Jamie, Dr. Smart is an authority on whatever.*

So, now when Jamie encounters Dr. Smart at a conference or when he reads something that relates to Dr. Smart's project, Jamie can drop it in an envelope with a note saying this material made him think of Smart and his project and how it is going anyway?

It's nice when someone sets up the guidelines for a conversation, but with a little imagination, you'll be able to do that for yourself. The key is to focus on the other person.

Facilitate

Another way of staying in touch with colleagues is by being a facilitator; helping other people. If a casting director is looking for a particular type, don't be afraid to mention the best actor you can think of for the project. Remember the names of producers and directors, costumers and set designers. Be happy to share a terrific person you have worked with and suggest how she might solve somebody else's problem. If you can't remember names, keep notes and use them. What goes around comes around.

The Way It Really Is

Actors who have given up believing in fairy tales in real life still have a hard time letting go as far as the business is concerned. Me, too. I know the score and I *still* believe the movies. I still think that if I got an Academy Award nomination it would change my career. In fact, it would change my social status. But even that is *only* during the time between when the nominations come out and the winner is announced. A win is good for a few more months, but not much more.

The Los Angeles Times addressed the Oscar issue in an interesting article entitled, "Is Oscar Nomination a Career Boost?" written by Ellen Farley, March 30, 1988, regarding the women nominees for best supporting actresses,

• ...*ask the agents who represent these women about the impact of the nominations on their careers and it becomes clear that even the lustre of an Academy of Motion Picture Arts and Sciences Oscar nomination doesn't alter a movie business truism:*

'As we all know,' agent Susan Streitfeld lamented the other day, 'to be in this business you should be 21 and beautiful.'

Only Anne Archer, who plays younger than her 40 years and is drop-dead gorgeous in her nominated role as the good wife and mother in "Fatal Attraction", claims to be rolling in scripts.

But Archer's situation is in sharp contrast to that of other nominees.

I have watched friends of mine win awards with varying results.

The plain facts are that awards, by and large, are economic considerations that only incidentally benefit the actor. They were instituted originally to draw attention to the projects of the producers. Today the sponsors of such ceremonies use them not only to promote their industry, but to gain large television revenues for the awards ceremony.

A Tony is very prestigious within the

Broadway theater community and will certainly get you considered for more parts. Two Tonys are worth a lot more than one and three are worth even more than that. They signify that you have become a bonafide member of the Broadway fraternity (notice that I did not say sorority, for it is still mainly a man's game). Employers in Los Angeles could not care less about Broadway awards unless the winners were in some huge international success that gained great media attention.

One Emmy was thrilling for a friend of mine. But it was only after the second win that she moved up to become a member of the hierarchy. She still finds herself unemployed sometimes and she still loses out to performers of more 'visibility' but her status is forever changed and she can command more money.

The Academy Award is still the most prestigious award, but I can't remember who won last year, can you? I don't care. I still want one. I think winning an award would make most of us heady:

Look! I've been voted on by a jury of my peers!

Oh yeah?

I go to those Academy screenings and the selections for some awards totally baffle me because I know not that many people saw those screenings, at least not at the Motion Picture Academy. Maybe they all have private screen-ing rooms?

Because of the vast amount of television product, the members of the Television Academy can't possibly see everything and few take it seriously enough to vote only for those performances they see. I know all these things. Do you really think I will remember them if I'm ever nominated?

The whole awards process mostly puts actors in a cranky mood. When you spend your whole life thinking one of these events is going to change your standing in the business and it doesn't, it's disappointing. Actors tend to think, then, that all is lost.

Nothing is any more lost than it was the day before. You are not a better or worse actor because you were or were not nominated or did or did not win. Just think of it as your birthday. If you are lucky, on your birthday, people treat you very well. Then, the next day, it isn't your birthday. You are able to accept that and it's very similar.

Rags to Riches and Back Again

Henry Winkler had to hitchhike to the audition for "Happy Days." He was, in fact, picked up by one of the people who ended up hiring him. Henry was young and made it big.

Danny DeVito and Rhea Perlman lived in a one room apartment for 15 years in New York before they began to work with any regularity for money.

As wonderful as it is to finally 'make it,' it's just as depressing when casting directors and producers decide an actor is overexposed. The actor can then go from being a household name to being totally unemployed for years.

Howard Keel, who was a huge star 30 years ago on Broadway and in MGM musicals, told me an interesting story at a dinner party. When musicals went out of business, so did Keel and he spent years unemployed and depressed. He finally gave up and decided to move to Oklahoma City and get into the oil business. He considered himself a failure when he hired the truck and left California. In true Hollywood style, as soon as he had accepted his new lifestyle, the phone call came that put him back to work on the hit television series, "Dallas"

My own choice of acting was not based in any way on the reality of what the life is really about. Actually, it may have been based on what the life was about when I was five years old, but the business is totally different today than it was then.

It is even different today than it was in 1980. At that time, there was a long actors strike that had profound effects on the industry. Actually, I don't think the actors strike that changed the business. The strike only reflected the changes that had already occurred in the industry and the world.

For whatever reason, since that time there has been much less product; there are far fewer jobs for everyone. Smaller parts that would have gone to actors with no 'name value' are now taken by stars.

Parts on episodes once available to the working actor are now held back for actors who are already employed on nighttime series. The result is that for other than star film actors and actors regularly employed in very successful nighttime shows, it is more difficult than usual.

What Have You Been Doing?

There's a wonderful joke about the actor who was found in bed with another man's wife. The irate husband demanded,

What have you been doing?

The actor struck a pose, scratched his head and

recounted,

A recurring part in "Home Front", two shots on "LA Law" and a TV movie.

Most of the time, when someone asks an actor that question, they want to know, *Are you working as an actor?* I'm instantly guilty when someone asks me the question and I'm not working. It doesn't matter that I might have written four books, gone to China, volunteered at the hospital and saved four people from a burning building. Nothing seems to counts but working as an actor.

I *never* ask a friend if she has been working and I *never* tell her if I have been. First of all, I figure that if she has been working, it will 'come out' in conversation. Secondly, if I have been working and she hasn't, I don't want to make her feel uncomfortable. If it becomes apparent that we have both been working or that we are both not working, then we can discuss the business, but I'd rather talk about something else.

Civilians, of course, do not understand. When I lived in New York, I did a great many commercials, but like everyone else, I went through dry periods without much on the air. During a particularly depressing time, one of the people in my apartment building (whom I didn't know) greeted me warmly and said,

Say, haven't seen you on the tube lately. Have you left the business?

No, I wanted to scream at him, *I feel like the business has left me.*

You are not paranoid. Your worst nightmares are true. If you are not currently working (visible), everyone concludes that you are dead and out of the business. Let this be their problem, don't buy into that thinking for yourself. You are only 'out of work': You have been given a gift of time to study, do your Christmas shopping or get married before your next job. You are neither dead and out of the business nor an 'unemployed actor' who suspects he will never work again - if he ever did. The way you choose to think about periods of not working will make a profound difference in your life. There *will* be times (sometimes *long* times) when you will not work. If you choose to stay home and eat, sleep, cry, drink or any of 100 other self destructive choices available, instead of making your own work and/or getting on with you life, you will be missing out on time that could be productive and happy.

In order to work it is true that you will have to be a persistent *detective* to find the job and a *press agent* to capitalize on your good fortune. You must have the courage and nerve of a *gambler* to negotiate your contracts and also to take a chance doing something original at an audition. Only a gambler would stay in a business when it seems as though the odds are against you (and they always are). You must constantly *study* to refine your craft, you must be an *entrepreneur* to create your own work, whether you become a book reviewer, *a director*, a *producer,* a *teacher,* do *stand-up* or any of the other actor options within the field. You must have the character insights of a *psychologist* not only to break down a character, but to understand basic human behavior (yours as well as the person you are dealing with) and surely you will have to become a *philosopher* in order to put all this in a proper perspective.

If you are a smart actor, you will not allow success to stifle these gifts. Actors frequently believe that a measure of success brings freedom from the entrepreneurial aspects of the work. When we become concerned with protecting position and status and lose touch with our own action and vision, work frequently dries up.

Systems Dynamics Exchange

There's a fascinating engineering theory my son explained to me. It has to do with systems/dynamics/ exchange. The principle can be demonstrated with my furnace. When I turn up the thermostat in my house, it takes a few moments for the furnace to kick on. It takes even longer for my house to warm up. Therefore, if I'm smart, I will turn on the thermostat before I am cold. So it is with our careers, getting lazy frequently means getting left out in the cold.

More stuff for your notebook:

✓   auditioning
       preparation
       choosing material
       behavior
       insecurity
       waiting
✓   negotiating
✓   getting replaced
✓   stars
✓   getting hired
✓   being 'right'
✓   professional behavior

- ✓ networking
- ✓ facilitating
- ✓ reality
- ✓ awards
- ✓ rags to riches
- ✓ systems dynamics exchange

Whew! It must be time to talk about *agents!*

- 10 -
Agents

At the beginning of my career, I thought if I got the right theatrical agent, he could/would make me a star. I thought agents had the power of making or breaking your career. I knew this wasn't true in the commercial field because when I did commercials back home in Texas, I had learned how to call on film companies and advertising agencies myself. That meant I didn't feel so dependent on agents for this service since I had already been successful and had a reel of commercials to show. I felt I was at least employable.

Although I had no idea how a theatrical agent would receive me, my previous experience had taught me to be businesslike about calling on agents. I told myself I could not eat lunch until I had visited at least one theatrical agent. I would get myself up for it by telling myself if I did not go in and leave a picture and resume I had *no* chance. But if I left a picture and resume, the agent would be aware of my existence, at least, and my chances would improve. But after all my 'late' lunches, it was through a commercial agent that I got the break that gave me credibility with theatrical agents. Estelle Tepper (now a casting director in Los Angeles) was working in a New York talent agency that submits for both commercial *and* theatrical projects. One day, she had the opportunity to submit actors for a film the whole city was working on entitled "The Gap." I'm pretty sure she must have emptied out her drawer and submitted every actor she had who was the right color and within 10

years of being the right age.   Regardless, that is how
Peter Boyle, Dennis Patrick, Audrey Caire and I came
to be cast in a film that was listed on many '10 best'
lists for 1971. The movie, Susan Sarandon's first
film, was released with a new title: "Joe."

After the film and some very nice reviews
came out, I still didn't choose an agent. In New York
it's easy to exist working freelance and I was so
frightened of choosing the wrong agent that I didn't
choose one at all.   Finally, the late Jay Wolfe, a
wonderfully kind and talented casting director said,

K, you have *to choose an agent.   It just doesn't look
good not to be signed.*

Do you know what I did? I chose a manager (and
gave away 15% more of my money - even on the
commercial business I had built myself) just because I
was afraid of choosing the wrong agent.

As I look back on it, I realize I wanted to
believe that some omnipotent person was going to step
in and move my theatrical career along for me just as I
had done for myself with my commercial career in
Texas. Well, the theatrical career was going to take
the same time and hard work and frankly, William
Morris was just not going to be interested at this
embryonic point.

It's frustrating, but understandable, that
credible agencies (who are not in the business of
starting careers) don't want you until you have done
all the groundwork that demonstrates your 'employ-
ability' by finding a way into the business on whatever
level. You must become so marketable that you are
able to attract an agent whose contacts coupled with
the actor's growing reputation result in a job or an

audition for one. Even Mike Ovitz (the head of Los Angeles' most powerful agency, Creative Artists Agency (CAA), can't sell a turkey. He might be able to force someone to take you, but why would he want to?

Although the agent is very important, he can only sell a marketable product. That means that the actor must maintain his physical appearance, deal optimistically with unemployment and aging and preserve his emotional health in an atmosphere that seems to thrive on pulling him down.

Even though I've been in the business over 20 years and I know all this, it's still a temptation to place too much emphasis on my agent. I want to believe he is getting, or not getting me, appointments. That way, when I'm not going out, it must be his responsibility.

It's not.

Again, acting is not about being chosen. It has to be about the work. The actor must get fulfillment from the work. If you do what you love fully, in a concentrated and committed fashion, you already have your reward, no matter what. If you work to get chosen, you will have a more difficult time distilling your essence, you will burn yourself out constantly second guessing the marketplace and worse, you will be perpetually disappointed.

If you look in any analytical way at someone's career, you will see a body of work that is supported (by and large) by good health (mental and physical), a strong sense of identity and self-confidence coupled with shrewd business savvy.

You will hear of an actor who just walked in off the street and became a BIG STAR. Television series and films can quickly make incredible stars that are so huge that you (and *they*) can't believe they will ever be out of work again. They will.

Was anybody ever as big as "The Fonz" (Henry Winkler) when "Happy Days" was big? If Winkler hadn't been able to hold onto his perspective and perfect other talents during his tenure of being hot, he could be sitting home today with all his TV Guide covers instead of directing and producing. And where *is* Erik Estrada?

Agents are not the solution to the puzzle, but they are part of the equation. Interestingly enough, they consider us the other part. And what are they looking for?

The Definitive Client

• *I want to know either they work and make a lot of money so that I can support my office or that the potential to make money is there. I am one of the people who goes for talent, so I do take people who are not big money makers, because I am impressed with talent.*

      Martin Gage
      The Gage Group, Los Angeles

• *More jobs are available for certain types of actors than other types so you look at the physicality. For that look you know can sell. And nine times out of ten, that look is gorgeous. Men. Women. Beautiful. It's just a fact.*

      Ric Beddingfield
      J. Michael Bloom, Ltd., Los Angeles

• *I love a good resume. Even if there is no TV and film, if someone has great training and practical experience, even if it's La Mirada Steak House Dinner Theater, it's nice to see that. Some people make up video tapes with monologues on it. It's nice when an actor comes in well-prepared. For example, if he's gotten key casting people to call me and networks his way into the office. I'm impressed with that.*

Daryl Marshak
Harry Gold and Associates, Los Angeles

• *I like an actor who, when he hits the door, is competing. Some people are afraid to ask for what they want. You can ask for anything. It's all in knowing how to ask for it. I like an actor who has his own process. Maybe he reminds me of something I forgot to do.*

Ric Beddingfield
J. Michael Bloom, Ltd., Los Angeles

• *I want an actor with the ability to get a job and pay me a commission.*

Beverly Anderson
Beverly Anderson, New York City

• *My favorite kind of client? I like character actors. I like black actors and Hispanic actors very much. I understand them. I don't know why. We like developing people. We look at backgrounds. I like stage. I love people who do the footwork. When I see a blank resume and they say, 'I'm talented, trust me,' that's the kiss of death in this office. I can see when someone has gone through the theater department; someone has done a lot of Equity Waiver plays. I appreciate that. When someone tells me they study a lot, that*

kind of scares me. I think there's studying and there's practical experience.
> Daryl Marshak
> Harry Gold & Associates, Los Angeles

• *If they're a character actor, you have to ask yourself, 'Do I need another character actor in my life?' Or, if they're attractive, then you have to start praying they can act.*
> Ric Beddingfield
> J. Michael Bloom, Ltd., Los Angeles

New York agent Beverly Anderson told me about meeting a prospective client and her reaction to her.

• *Sigourney Weaver asked to come in and meet me when she was with a client of mine in Ingrid Bergman's show, "The Constant Wife." She's almost six feet tall. I'm very tall myself and when I saw her, I thought, 'God, honey, you're going to have a tough time in this business because you're so huge.' And she floated in and she did something no one had ever done. She had this big book with all her pictures from Bryn Mawr or Radcliffe of things she had done and she opened this book and she comes around and drapes herself over my shoulders from behind my chair and points to herself in these pictures. She was hovering over me. And I thought - - no matter what happens with me - - this woman is going to make it. There was determination and strength and self-confidence and positiveness. Nobody's ever done that to me before.*
> Beverly Anderson
> Beverly Anderson, New York City

• *Training is the most important thing. I get very annoyed with people. Someone is attractive, so people say, 'You should be in television,' and then the actor thinks that's going to just 'happen.'*

J. Michael Bloom
J. Michael Bloom, Ltd., Los Angeles

Audition Tape

A component that will get you in the door at almost any agency is an *audition tape.* You should put together a tape (no longer than ten minutes) as soon as you have any professional examples of your work. When you are just beginning, this might be several commercials (or moments from the commercials that feature you), a student film or even a non-union film. It can be two minutes or five, it doesn't have to be ten, but it should be something to show what you look like on film and give some idea of your range. This is a quick sales tool that can save you and the agent a lot of time.

A few years ago I received a frantic call from a woman who explained to me that she was enrolled in a seminar I was teaching that weekend for the American Film Institute, but that she needed me sooner. She had an appointment with an agent on Friday and she wanted to know if she could make an appointment for a consultation.

I told her to bring everything she had. Pictures, resumes, any examples of her work on film. She was about 35, overweight, blowzy, very nice. I looked at her film and suggested that she *NOT* go to the agent without a reel. We selected the scenes we felt were best and she rushed to have a tape made.

A week later, she called to tell me that when

she got to the agent's office, the agent seemed unim-
pressed and passed her off to her assistant. The
actress left her tape anyway. Over the weekend, she
discovered another piece of film that she wanted to
add to her tape. She called the agent's office to see if
they had looked at the tape. They hadn't gotten to it
yet and were annoyed that she had called. She explained that she had more film to add to it and that she
would like to come by, pick it up, add the tape and
return. There was a lot of sighing:

All right. Come and get it.

By the time the actress got there, the agent had looked
at the tape. She was welcomed warmly.

*Come in. Come in. We think you are wonderful.
Can we sign you?*

Without the tape, she would probably have been
passed over. It is pretty impossible to tell in an office
meeting whether or not you are a good actor or to
have any idea of someone's range.

    Producing a tape of yourself is often a waste of
money because most agents either will not look at a
home-produced tape or will not give it much
credibility. Therefore, one of your first goals should
be to amass professional work on film. Call every
theater and film school in your area and volunteer for
student films. Do what you can with commercials and
Industrial Film. This is an important entree into the
business.

So, agents are looking for:

training	commerciality
experience	presence
talent	attitude
looks	self-confidence
potential	competitiveness

Well, I'd like to find all those things in an agent.

The Definitive Agent

If Beverly Anderson looks mainly for an actor who can get the job, I think the actor has to be primarily looking for an agent who can get him the audition. That sounds pretty simple, doesn't it?

Maybe, but listen to New York agent, Marvin Starkman:

• *If the actor/agent relationship were based on getting auditions for everything, then the agent would have a right to say that you must get everything I send you out on. If you don't get everything I send you on, then we have a one-sided relationship.*

Getting an audition isn't necessarily the most important thing, either. Is he sending you on the right auditions? Does he see you accurately? Do you both have the same perception regarding the roles you are right for?

Los Angeles agent, Fred Amsel puts it another way:

• *The agent has to know what the actor can do - what the range is - so he knows how to handle that*

particular artist.
> Fred Amsel
> Amsel & Associates, Los Angeles

I asked agents what qualities they would look for if they were choosing agents. They mentioned integrity, client list, communication, background and taste.

To know whether an agent possesses these traits, you'll have to do some research. "Reel Power," written by Mark Litwak and published by William Morrow is not only an interesting read, but it delineates a whole raft of other ideas regarding qualifications for successful agents:

• *First, an agent must have the stamina to handle a heavy workload and be able to endure the frenetic pace in which business is conducted. 'It's like working in the commodities pit,' says William Morris agent Joan Hyler. 'It's hectic,' says agent Lisa Demberg, 'because you can't do your job unless you're always on the phone, always talking to someone, or socializing with someone or trying to do business, or following up on the projects you've discussed.'*
> *'Great agents,' says agent-turned-executive Stephanie Brody, 'have enthusiasm and tireless energy. And they must be efficient. The agent is juggling 30 phone calls a day. He has to send out material, and follow up. You have to be extremely well-organized.'*
> *Second, agents must be able to cope with the vicissitudes of the business. 'In a certain sense it's like 'Dialing for Dollars,' says William Morris agent Bobbi Thompson. 'Each call may be the big money. You never know. It's all a roulette wheel.'*
> *Third, an agent must be an effective salesman.*
> *Fourth, agents must be able to discern talent.*

Many top agents are very aggressive in their pursuit of deals - some would say ruthless. Says a former CAA agent, 'In order to be an extraordinarily successful agent you can't have any qualms about lying, cheating, stealing and being totally into yourself.'

Reel Power
Mark Litwak
William Morrow & Company, Inc.
New York, New York

I was particularly struck by what Joan Hyler said about agenting being like working in the commodities pit. Frequently there is no tangible reason why the commodities market goes up or down, just as there is frequently no tangible reason why one actor gets a job and the other one doesn't or why one actor is singled out by the public and another one isn't.

• *The winning difference between two actors on the same level auditioning for a role may just be that one makes everyone in the room have a better time.*

Barry Freed
Barry Freed Agency, Los Angeles

So much for talent and training.

• *One of the chief factors that determines the value of an agent is information. It is impossible for a small agent to possess the amount of information that a large agent can. We track hundreds of projects weekly at all of the studios and networks. If a client walks in and asks about a project, I can haul out 400 pages of notes and say, 'Oh yeah, it's at this studio and this is the producer and they're doing a rewrite right now and they're hoping to go with it on this date and talking to so-and-so about it.' I* have *that information.*

    Gene Parseghian
    Triad, New York

So, Gene thinks (I certainly agree) that information is important. Two other traits I want in an agent are:

Access and Stature

The dictionary defines *access* as 'ability to approach' or 'admittance.' In New York and Los Angeles, conglomerate agencies have so many stars on their lists, they have plenty of 'ability to approach.' If the studios, networks and producers do not return their phone calls, they might find the agency retaliating by withholding their important stars.

    Stature, on the other hand, is entirely different. Webster defines the word as 'level of achievement'. So, other prestigious, mid-level Los Angeles agents like Michael Bloom and Martin Gage surely have more *stature* than some lowly agent at William Morris, but possibly not as much *access*.

    There's also the question of *style*. I know an actor who had a very effective agent who yelled at everyone (the client and the casting directors). That's not to say the agent didn't get the actor appointments, he did. The actor simply decided that wasn't the way he wanted to be represented.

    In smaller marketplaces, the same qualifiers hold true. There may just be one agent in town for you to choose from, who may not have stature and/or access. Then you will have to acquire these attributes yourself. It's not impossible. We (and they) build credibility by telling the truth. By saying something and carrying through. Don't promise something you can't deliver. If you can get someone to see you and experience you and you have something to sell, they will hire you. Perhaps not today, but it will happen.

Size

When you are shopping for an agent, make sure you get one that is your size. The most effective formula is the agency with the smallest number of credible clients and the largest number of well-respected agents. Many agents believe a good ratio is one agent to 20-25 actors.

For a successful partnership, you and your agent must have the same goals and visions about you, your talent and your career. If you think you can be a star and your agent doesn't, it's a mutual waste of time and energy. If he thinks you can be a star and you aren't up for it, he's going to be very frustrated.

Aggressiveness and enthusiasm are part of the mix as well as (for me) integrity. In a fairy tale business, it's comforting and necessary to know that at least one person is telling you the truth.

So the chief factors to look for in an agent are stature and access, perception, compatibility, enthusiasm, aggressiveness, ratio of actors to agents, style, and integrity.

Let's say you have now landed the agent of your dreams (or the only agent in town). Now what?

The Relationship

All relationships take time, thought, creative energy and communication in order to be successful. This includes your relationship with your agent. As in other relationships, it is important to know what you want from the relationship in order to get it. Better to decide what you want *before* you sign a contract.

What are all the possible characteristics you might want from your relationship with your agent? There's a whole list of things I require.

It's important to me that my agent return my phone calls promptly. That might not be important to someone else, but it is high on my list of requirements.

I also want my agent to submit me for any job I am right for. I would like him to have the stature to get his phone calls returned from important casting directors. I want him to have the imagination and aggressiveness to suggest me for roles that might be terrific for me, though unusual casting-wise.

I think we all want to be able to communicate honestly and easily with our agent, but trust doesn't happen in a day, from either one of you. There IS going to be a period of getting acquainted and learning each other's signals. Don't be impatient. This person is your business partner. He needs to talk to you as much as you need to talk to him if he is going to represent you well.

Your agent doesn't have to be involved in your social circle, but he can be. Some people want their agents to console them when they're not working. If that is your need and your arrangement, fine, but it's really not part of the job description.

It's important to know what you want and communicate that information to your prospective business partner as well to find out what his needs are in order to negotiate the shape of your prospective partnership.

It's going to be a marriage, after all, so you will need to have the same goals, tastes, value system and vision regarding the possibilities of your union.

How Can I Get a Meeting?

The best way to contact an agent is through a referral. If you know someone on the agent's list who can act as a go-between, that is fine.

In New York or Los Angeles, if you know him well enough, you might ask a casting director you have worked with to make the phone call for you, but what if you don't have any of these entrees?

If you are young and beautiful, drop your picture off looking as Y&B as possible. If you are really Y&B and can speak at all, few will require you do much more. It's sad (for the rest of us), but true, so you may as well cash in on it. If you are smart, you will study while cashing. Y&B doesn't linger long and you may want to work during those grey years of your 30's and beyond.

As I mentioned earlier, I think it's best to send a letter a couple of days before sending a picture and resume. Letters get read while pictures and resumes tend to sit in the 'As Soon As I Get To It' stack. Address your letter to a specific agent, preferably one of the associates. They get less mail than the owner so you might get attention much sooner.

Remember, type your letter and use good paper. State that you are looking for representation and that you are impressed with the agency's client list (make sure you know who is on it) and that your credits compare favorably. Tell him your picture and resume will arrive in the next day's mail. Make sure it does. Do *not* say you want this person for your agent (you don't know that yet). Mention a few key credits. If your credits don't look that impressive, but you did work with Sir Olivier, by all means note that. If your letter has piqued interest, your picture will be opened immediately. Mail your letter so that it arrives on Wednesday or Thursday away from the first of the week rush. On Monday, not only is the agent catching up from the weekend, so it everyone else and his desk is full. If your letter arrives later in the week, it will have less competition. Your follow-up call (late afternoon is the best time) should be brief and upbeat. Be a person the agent wants to talk to. If he doesn't want a meeting, get over the disappointment and go on to the next agent on your list.

When Carol Burnett went to New York, agents said to call when she was 'in something'. Didn't they know if she was 'in something' that she wouldn't need an agent?

Finally, she enlisted her boyfriend (a writer) and the young women she lived with in a residence for young actresses. They produced their own show and invited all the agents in town. They all came!

When I interviewed New York agent Lionel Larner, (he's Glenda Jackson's and Carroll O'Connor's agent) he told me,

• *Tell actors to produce something in their living room and invite agents. I would come.*

There really is an agent for everyone, even in New York and Los Angeles. Your focus, energy and attitude can put you ahead of the pack. If you are committed, shoulder your responsibilities, do the work and pursue employment in a professional manner, you will prosper.

The Meeting

Okay, you've got an appointment. Now what will you do? How will you dress? How will you behave? What questions should you ask?

Polish your shoes and look terrific. It is a job interview, after all. I attended a seminar conducted by a famous corporate job counsellor. She said the number one thing employers notice before all else is whether or not shoes are scuffed. In every business, employers make judgements they don't even know they are making. It's unconscious, but part of the over all effect that makes a positive or negative impact. Remember how impressed you are by style and how turned off you are by the lack of it. The agent feels the same. In today's world, packaging is everything. Content is important, but the first impression is still the first impression. Be yourself. Be natural and forthright. Don't talk too much. Ask questions, but not right away. First, you both need to get comfortable. I can't stress this strongly enough. You don't want to waste each other's time, but a little give-and-take about the weather, the earthquake, the World Series or one of his clients that you admire, will give you each time to settle the natural adrenalin spurt that happens in an unfamiliar circumstance. This will give you a chance to view each other's persona. It's like any other first date; you're both trying to figure out if you want a second one. Although you are there to present yourself to the agent, he's the salesman, after all so don't tell him he could make a lot of money on you. Agents have told me such self-serving remarks automatically conclude the meeting. He's not the agent for you if he can't figure that out by your presence and credits.

This is the time for clarity. Tell him you think you are due for a series, a film or whatever, but be realistic. Ask what he thinks is your realistic next step, tell him what you think your strongest points are.

Learn how the office works. If you're being interviewed by the owner, is he going to work for you or is he just the charmer? I know actors who signed with agencies because they were impressed with the owner, but after becoming clients, he rarely crossed their path.

Are you welcome to call? Can you drop by the office? Should you call first? Will the agents come to see your work? Will they consult you before they turn down work? Are they good about returning phone calls? Explore your own feelings about these issues before you arrive.

If you need to be able to talk regularly to your agent, now's the time to mention it. He needs to know that's one of the things you require. You might want to ask if the office has a policy of regularly requesting audition material for clients at least a day in advance of the audition. Let him know your requirements to present yourself at your best. If that turns him off, this isn't the agent for you.

Isn't it nice to know there are specific things on your mind to ask about during the meeting so you won't just sit there quaking and hoping to be chosen? Remembering how overeager people turn you off may help your perspective in these meetings. Remember, what you don't ask today can come back to haunt you tomorrow.

So, you were on time. You did not arrive with an unattractive attitude. You met. You asked questions. You were respectful. You have acted naturally.

Now, be the one to end the meeting. Make it clear you value the agent's time and you know it is a precious commodity. He will appreciate that. Suggest you both think about the meeting for a day or two and then decide. Be definite about when you will get back to him (it should be less than a week). You may have other agents to meet. Mention this. If he's last on the list, mention you have to go home and digest all the meetings. Then go home and do just that. Let him know you were pleased with the meeting. Even if it wasn't your finest moment, or his, be gracious. After all, you each did your best.

I advise a 24-hour fantasy-shakedown period. When I was interviewing all 200+ agents for my Los Angeles book, I wanted every agent I talked to while I was there (they are salesmen, after all). After a cooling-off period, I found my feelings to be more realistic. The hyperbole seemed to have drifted out of my head and I was able to assess more clearly what went on.

It is important to jot down your feelings and thoughts about each meeting as soon as you get home. Then, look at all the notes the next day and reevaluate your feelings. Never forget you are choosing an agent. The qualities you look for in a friend are not necessarily qualities you desire in an agent.

Now you are ready to digest all your research and make a decision. You've done the hard part.

I heard a story about director, Mike Nichols. He was giving a speech to the actors on opening night:

• *Just go out there and have a good time. Don't let it worry you that __The New York Times__ is out there; that every important media person in the world is watching you; that we've worked for days and weeks and months on this production; that the investors are going to lose their houses if it doesn't go well; that the writer will commit suicide and that this could be the end of your careers if you make one misstep. Just go out there and have a good time.*

I think this is the way many of us feel about choosing an agent. We act as if it is a momentous decision having irrevocable consequences on our careers.

It's not. You can get a job without an agent. An agent can't book a job without an actor. Keep things in perspective. Do the research, weigh the evidence, then make the decision. The successful career is built on self-knowledge.

Trust your instincts. You already know what to do. Do it.

The Partnership

Once you have chosen the agent, visit him to sign contracts and meet (and fix in your mind) all auxiliary people in your new office.

If there are several, note who is who and where they sit, as soon as you leave the office. Until you become more familiar with everyone, you can consult your map before each subsequent visit.

Leave a good supply of pictures and resumes. If you are in Los Angeles or New York, leave videocassette tapes (if you have them), as well as a list of casting directors, producers and directors with whom you have relationships. Alphabetize the list if you ever want the agent to use it. Keep abreast of projects so that the next time Steven Spielberg has a project, you can remind your agent that you and Steven went to school together. After all, he has lots of clients.

Also leave a list of your quotes (how much you were paid for your last jobs in theatre, film and television), plus information on billing. The more background you give your agent, the better he can represent you. If it's a large office, leave *each agent* your quotes and relationship information.

90% / 10%

Now the real work begins. Remember the agent only gets 10% of the money. You can't really expect him to do 100% of the work.

It's time for you to focus on your expectations. If you don't want him to be lazy, set a good example. Let him see how hard you are working to perfect and sell yourself. Let him see how enthusiastic you are. He will take his cue from you.

It's similar to one's relationship to his children. If you have a positive view of life and act on it, the chances are that your children will, also. If your children see you taking care of business, that's the norm. How you and your agent function together is a joint work in progress to which you will both contribute. I don't want to suggest that you can reform anyone's character, I'm assuming that with your diligence and investigation, you have already chosen a like-minded agent.

We hope agents are going to initiate work for us and introduce us to casting directors, producers, directors, etc., but their real contribution over a career span is negotiating, making appointments for us, being supportive in our dark moments and helping us retain our perspective in the bright moments.

Give a good agent a real 'career' to work with

and watch him build the momentum. Even then, successful actors don't just hand it all over. They continue to do 90% of the work.

What Does *That* Mean?

Your agent's job is to get the buyer enthusiastic about you. Your job once you get an agent is to keep your agent enthusiastic about you.

When I finally signed with an agent in New York, after successfully freelancing for a long time, I thought my part of the hustling was over. When I consider how much I might have contributed to my career if I had agented more, I'm pretty startled. My brain could have been teeming with all kinds of possibilities if I had even begun to think this way. It never even occurred to me that my agent might forget about me.

Consider this. If someone came into the room right now, gave you a script to read and then asked for your casting suggestions, who would you be able to think of? My bet is the list would be heavy with the actors you have just seen in a movie, on television, stage or in person. Is your agent any different?

Actor's Responsibilities

I know actors who are angry when they have to tell their agents how to negotiate for them. They feel the agent is not doing his job if he has to be reminded to go for a particular kind of billing or per diem or whatever. If the agent has it all together and does everything perfect, that's great, but it's your career. It's up to you to know what the union minimums are, how you go about getting more money and who else might be getting it. You are getting the 90%.

Not only is it your responsibility to have your own plan for your career, it's a way for you to be in control of your destiny in a business where it is all too easy to feel tossed about by the whims of the gods.

It's your vision and your focus that have gotten the agent's interest in the first place. Why would you want to hand over your business to someone else? The larger the support system and the more sources of energy focusing on a single goal, the larger the payoff. You can't afford to give up your role as your agent.

If you are looking for an agent in the Los Angeles or New York area, buy either *The New York Agent Book* or *The Los Angeles Agent Book* for specific information regarding researching these marketplaces and more detailed information regarding agent/actor relationships.

So write in your book that when looking for an agent, remember these things:

✓ the relative value of agents
✓ self-agenting
✓ the definitive client
✓ the definitive agent
✓ audition tapes
✓ it's a relationship
✓ know your requirements
✓ communication
✓ how to get a meeting
✓ what to do when you get there
✓ it's a partnership
✓ 90%-10%
✓ your responsibilities

Now let's talk about unions.

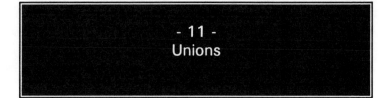

When I was as aspiring actor, my goal was to join
Actors Equity. I decided that when I got my Equity
card, *then* I would be an actor. I got my SAG card
first, but that was through commercials, so in my
mind, it didn't count because Equity was my goal.
And I *did* feel like I was a real actor when I got into
Equity. I wasn't any different from the day before,
but I felt different and that *is* worth a lot, just like the
Cowardly Lion getting 'courage' with a medal in the
"Wizard of Oz".

One's image of oneself not-with-standing, it is
not always a good idea to join a union until you really
have to. On any given day, of the 78,000 actors who
are already members of Screen Actors Guild, only
11,700 (15%) are working. If you are not a member
of the union, at least all those more experienced actors
with better credits are not your competition. There
are many non-union jobs available that might net you
some work. Since the pay is low or non-existent,
those out of work union actors (who have already done
the groundwork you are now involved in) would not
be interested.

Non-union jobs include not only features with
no union connection, but films for student film-makers
(they may be at regular colleges or in prestigious film
schools like the American Film Institute, The
University of Southern California, The New York
Film School, etc.), or documentaries, government and
educational films.

Investigate the project to see if it is worthwhile, but even a bad film will teach you a lot. You will see yourself on film, be on a set, watch set-ups and learn to get along with people in unpleasant and stressful situations. Use discretion, Traci Lords not withstanding, sleezo film will not enhance your repertoire.

Earlier we spoke of the actor's *Catch-22:* You have to have a job to get into the union, but you can't get a job without a union card. Once you are a member of *any* of the performer unions, you may not work non-union in the jurisdiction of *any* of the unions involved in the Association of Actors and Artists of America if any of those unions are trying to organize the project you are considering.

If you are in Los Angeles, read <u>Drama-Logue</u> for casting news for projects. In New York, read <u>Backstage</u> and <u>Show Business</u>. If you are in smaller marketplaces, check any university or school where students are involved in film. Read the classifieds. Be alert. Keep the word out when you are in theater circles that you are looking for these opportunities.

When It's Time

There are three main performers' unions:

o   Actors Equity Association (AEA/Equity)
o   American Federation of Television and Radio Artists (AFTRA)
o   Screen Actors Guild (SAG)

Equity

AEA (or Equity as it is commonly known) is the labor

union encompassing all professional performers in legitimate theater in the United States. Equity administers contracts on Broadway, touring productions, Bus and Truck tours, Resident Dramatic Stock, Non-Resident Dramatic Stock, Indoor Musical Stock, Outdoor Musical Stock, Dinner Theaters, League of Resident Theaters (LORT), Industrial Shows, Theater for Young Audiences, Off-Broadway, Hollywood Area Theaters (HAT), Bay Area Theaters (BAT), Chicago Area Theaters (CAT), University Theaters, Outdoor Drama Festivals and Cabaret Theater.

There are three ways to become a member of Equity:

1. By signing an Equity contract with a producer in any branch of the union's jurisdiction.

2. If you are a member of and *have been* employed under the jurisdiction of the 'sister unions' i.e., American Federation of Television and Radio Artists, American Guild of Musical Artists, American Guild of Variety Artists, Screen Actors Guild, Screen Extras Guild, Association Puertoriquenta de Artistas y Technicos Del Espectaculo [APATE], Italian Actors Unions [IAU], and Hebrew Actors Unions [HAU].

Applicants must be members in good standing of the parent union for one year to be eligible for membership in Equity and must have performed under the jurisdiction of the parent union as either a principal performer or have three days of work comparable to an extra performer on a non-waiver basis. Proof of membership under SAG, AGMA or HAU is accepted by presenting a current membership card.

If the parent union is AFTRA, SEG or AGVA,

additional proof of employment is necessary.

3. Membership Candidate Program. After securing a non-professional position at a participating theater, the actor must register as an Equity Membership Candidate by completing the Equity non-professional affidavit and paying a registration fee. This one-time fee is credited against the initiation fee that becomes due upon joining the union. This program is in effect in Equity Resident Theaters, Dinner Theaters, Chicago Area Theaters and in Resident and Non-Resident Dramatic Stock.

After 50 weeks of work at accredited theaters, the Candidate is eligible for Equity membership. These 50 weeks need not be consecutive and may be accumulated over any period of time.

AEA Fees & Dues

Initiation fee is currently $800, payable prior to election to membership. Basic dues are $37 twice a year. Additionally, there are working dues: 2% of gross weekly earnings from employment. This 2% is deducted from your check before you receive it in the same way your income tax is deducted.

As I mentioned above, there are many different contracts which cover the spectrum of theatrical employment. I'm including a few contracts (all prices quoted are weekly) just to give you an idea. Call your local Equity office for specific contracts.

Non-Resident Musical & Dramatic
Stock (Council of Stock Theaters or COST)/$476.06

Non-Resident Dramatic Stock
(over 800 seats)/ $518.36

Production Contract (Broadway, Jones Beach,
Etc.)/$900

Theater for Young Audiences (YTA contract)/$275

Equity Offices

Actors Equity Association (National Office)
165 West 46th Street
New York, NY 10036
212-869-8530

Actors Equity Association
7065 Hollywood Blvd.
Hollywood, CA 90028
213-856-6805

Branch offices are located in Chicago, Los Angeles
and San Francisco. Equity telephone lines in Atlanta,
Boston, Cleveland, Dallas/Ft. Worth, Detroit,
Houston, Kansas City, Miami, Minneapolis/St. Paul,
Philadelphia, St. Louis, San Diego, Seattle,
Washington/Baltimore.

AFTRA

The easiest union to get into is the American Federation of Television and Radio Artists (AFTRA).
AFTRA's jurisdiction covers live and taped television,
radio, transcriptions, phonograph records and non-
broadcast recorded material. Basically all you have to
do is pay the money, fill out the forms and you are a

member. If you are just buying your way into a union (that means there is no job involved) AFTRA will attach a rider to be signed by the performer acknowledging that *no work and/or access* to the other 4-A's (sister) Unions is automatically provided through the membership.

AFTRA Dues & Fees

The initiation fee is $800. Dues are payable semi-annually and are based on the performer's gross earnings under AFTRA's jurisdiction for the previous year. The lowest amount of annual dues (on earnings up to $2,000) is $84. If you make over $100,000, you pay $1,000.

AFTRA minimum is still being negotiated as I write this but is currently $306 a day for a commercial.

For taped syndicated shows other than commercials, the fee is $448 for ten half-hours over a two-day period. That means they can call you at any time over a 48 hour period and have you work 2 hours and then come back in 4 hours and work for 30 minutes until the job is finished or the ten half-hours are used up. Then they go into overtime. The half-hours do not have to be consecutive. Wonder why AFTRA is an unpopular union?

Nighttime rates for primetime are on a parity with Screen Actors Guild (see their rates). Day rates for soap operas are $402 for a principal role on a half-hour show (based on a 9 hour workday) and $536 for a one hour show. There is also a category for performers who speak five lines or less (frequently referred to as *five or under)*. It pays $190 for a half-hour show and $234 for an hour show.

There are special categories and different fees for announcers, newscasters, singers, chorus, etc., as well as radio and voice over. The fees I am quoting are for straight on-camera acting.

AFTRA Offices

American Federation of Television & Radio Artists
260 Madison Ave. (National Office)
New York, NY 10016
212-532-0800

American Federation of Television and Radio Artists
6922 Hollywood Blvd., P. O. Box 4070
Hollywood, CA 90078
213-461-8111

Screen Actors Guild

The most sought after union card is Screen Actors Guild (SAG). Actors may join SAG upon proof of employment or prospective employment within two weeks or less by a SAG-signatory film, television program or commercial. Proof of employment may be in the form of a signed contract, a payroll check or check stub, or a letter from the company (on company letterhead stationery). The document proving employment must state the applicant's name, Social Security number, the name of the production or commercial, the salary paid in dollar amount and the dates worked.

If you are a paid-up member of an affiliated performers' union (4-A's), for a period of at least one year *and* have worked at least once as a principal performer in that union's jurisdiction, you are eligible to join SAG.

SAG Dues & Fees

Initiation fee is 904.50. This includes the first semi-annual dues of $42.50. This is payable in full, in cashier's check or money order, at the time of application. The fees may be lower in some branch areas. SAG dues are based on SAG earnings and are billed twice a year.

Basic annual dues are $85. In addition, those members earning more than $5,000 annually under SAG contracts will pay 1½% of all money earned in excess of $5,000 up to a maximum of $150,000.

SAG Minimum for a day of work is $466 daily and $1620 weekly.

SAG Offices

Screen Actors Guild
7065 Hollywood Blvd.
Hollywood, CA 90028
213-465-4600

Screen Actors Guild
1515 Broadway, 44th Floor
New York, NY 10036
212-944-1030

SAG has branch offices in Atlanta, Boston, Chicago, Cleveland, Dallas, Denver, Detroit, Coral Gables, Honolulu, Houston, Minneapolis/St. Paul, Nashville, New York City, Philadelphia, Phoenix, St. Louis, San Diego, San Francisco, Seattle and Washington, DC.

The Union publishes an informative free booklet available to young SAG members called the AFTRA-SAG Young Performers Handbook. This

booklet defines young performers' rights in great
detail, as well as provides information for parents on
how to best fulfill their roles in their child's career.

Parent Union/Union Function

Whichever union the actor joins first is designated the
Parent Union.

As in any large collective of disparate parts,
there is frequently a great deal of grousing from
members regarding their unions. SAG members have
considerable internal dissension and the union threatens
to break apart from time to time.

Equity was embroiled in disputes over casting
in the Broadway hit: "Miss Saigon". Those disputes
were not only with the employers, but were a source
of strife between members of the union.

AFTRA faced a hard decision recently when
they decided to vote with Screen Actors Guild in
establishing jurisdiction over extras.

In spite of the exasperating politics, unions fill
an important need for actors. Powerless in many
situations, the actors are at least protected in the areas
of basic working conditions. The unions provide
hospitalization for their members, keep track of
residuals and are very helpful when an actor has any
kind of problem, particularly financial. There are
loans and grants available to members in time of need.
In addition, SAG, Equity, and AFTRA all are
participating in a work program to help non-working
members educate themselves to change careers if they
are interested.

It's easy to take these things for granted and
bad mouth the union when something does not go your
way and you have not bothered to get the facts.

Sometimes union members stab themselves in the back by working 'non-union' jobs hoping that the union will never find out. Sometimes union members work 'non-union' unknowingly because they have not checked to see if the employer is a signatory to a basic contract with the union. Just because there is a major advertising agency or a visible star involved doesn't necessarily mean the job is union sanctioned.

Be diligent, for the union rules are very clear: a union member is not allowed financial gain from a non-union job. The union will bring you up on charges and fine you the amount of money you made on the job *even if you thought the job was within the jurisdiction of the union.* Therefore, it pays to make a simple phone call.

There are many points to be made here.

First of all, it is the actor's responsibility to call the union and find out if the producers have in fact signed an agreement with the union. Stationery stores sell blank Screen Actors Guild contracts, so just because you sign a form that says Screen Actors Guild, and the employer pays SAG rates, doesn't mean there is an agreement in force.

Secondly, when you work a non-union job, there is no protection of basic working conditions, no contributions to health and welfare on the actors behalf (and therefore no hospitalization) and no guarantee of payment. When a producer makes an agreement with the unions, he puts up a bond guaranteeing the actor's salary.

Thirdly, hospitalization, decent pay, residuals, guaranteed meal times and overtime, have all been won from the employers over a long period of time through difficult negotiations. If you give these things away, you undermine the union and our collective bargaining agreements.

Last but not least, the union will most likely find out if you work non-union and you will be brought up on charges, possibly put on probation, fined and/or excluded from the union.

If you are not far along enough in your career to hold out for union jobs, don't join the union. If you *are* a professional, act like one. Live up to your responsibility by checking the status of projects you are considering.

Regardless of your union affiliation and jurisdiction, become an active member of your union. Too many of us become busy working and never take the time to go to meetings, become informed regarding the issues, join committees and become part of the policy making team. This frequently leaves the power to people who are not working the contracts to make the rules regarding the contracts. They are looking for ways to fill their time and although they have good intentions, they are making rules they will not be bound by, you will. Unless you are willing to spend some time contributing, you have no right to complain.

When you join, become active. Read the literature and become aware of the issues. Know what minimum is. Know what isn't working in your current contract. Form an idea about what would make things better, then go to a meeting or write a letter and work to put those plans into action.

Join any local professional organization of actors. It's not only a support group, it also looks good on your resume. Take your place within the ranks of your own profession.

The unions are as weak or as strong as the members. My own opinion is that there should be more stringent rules for membership that would take into consideration such things as training, apprenticeship and hours spent in the business. These types of rules govern craft unions such as hair and make-up.

Although it is difficult for a newcomer to join, there continue to be countless chronically non-working actors who are already union members. It is useless and expensive to join until you train yourself and have the tools (resume, craft and experience) to realistically expect employment.

When you join the union, vow to be an active, informed member. It's not always easy to obey rules others have made. This is your profession. Have pride in your union.

Notebook fodder about unions:

✓   non-union jobs can help get credibility
✓   don't join until marketable
✓   be an informed and active member

Children have no business giving up their childhoods to be actors. They are not in a position to make such a costly judgement about their lives. You only get to be a kid once. If you don't embrace childhood at the appropriate time, you will never get a legitimate shot at it again.

I urge any parent who is considering letting their child earn some 'easy' money to 'pay for their college tuition' with a few commercials and then, maybe an episode or two on television or maybe even a play, to really think again. Management pays a child as much money per day as an adult and expect the child to perform as an adult, no matter what. And what if things get out of hand and your child becomes the new Macauley Caulkin, can you or your child turn your back on all that money and adulation just so little Jimmy can play football and be a normal kid?

If your child is serious about pursuing a career in show business, encourage him to exercise his entrepreneurial skill as well as studying acting, so that when he gets out of school, he will be prepared. If he wants it *so much*, it will still be there when he is older. The newspapers are full of the publicized troubles of visible ex-child stars who will never get their 'lives' back again. It's a terrible chance to take.

If I you are a parent reading this and I cannot dissuade you from taking this tack, at least, let me give you some information regarding child labor laws as specified in the California Labor Code. If you live in another state, you might want to use this as your guide. It is up to *you* to protect your child. All management cares about is getting the film in the can.

Working Hours

• *The number of hours minors are permitted at the place of employment within a 24-hour period is limited according to age. Travel time must be considered working time.*

Babies under fifteen days old are not permitted to work.

Babies fifteen days old to six months may be on the set no more than two hours, but may work no more than twenty minutes.

Six months to two years may be on the set for four hours, but may work no more than two hours, the balance of time reserved for rest and recreation.

Two years to six years may be on the set for six hours, but may work no more than three hours, the balance reserved for rest and recreation.

Six years to nine years may be on the set for nine hours. When school is in session, they may work only four hours and must receive three hours of schooling with one hour for rest and recreation. When school is not in session, they may work six hours, the balance to be used for rest and recreation.

From nine to sixteen years may be on the set for nine hours. When school is in session, they may work five and must receive three hours of schooling, the balance being rest and recreation. When school is not in session, they may work seven hours, the balance for rest and recreation.

From sixteen to eighteen years may be on the set for ten hours. When school is in session, they may work six hours and must receive three hours of schooling, the balance for rest and recreation. When school is not in session, they may work eight hours, the balance for rest and recreation.

All minors under sixteen years of age: A studio teacher must be provided and has the responsibility for caring and attending to the health, safety and morals of the minor. For babies fifteen days to six weeks, a nurse must be present. A parent or guardian must be present on the set or location.

All minors under eighteen years of age must have a permit to work issued by the Labor Commissioner and their employers must also obtain a permit to employ. These permits are not required if the minor is sixteen or seventeen and is a high school graduate and has a certificate of proficiency.

California laws apply when a California employer takes a resident minor out of state.

The hours at the place of employment as shown above may be extended by no more than one-half hour for meal periods.

Twelve hours must elapse between the minor's time of dismissal and time of call on the following day.

For purposes of the California labor code, the entertainment industry is defined as 'any organization, or individual, using the services of any minor in: motion pictures of any type, (film, videotape, etc.) using any format (theatrical, film, commercial, documentary, television program, etc.) photography; recording; theatrical productions; publicity; rodeos; circuses; musical performances; and any other *performances where minors perform to entertain the public.'*

"Baby Talk" -
David Robb
Variety
June 26, 1991

Managers

Although I am usually not a supporter of having a manager, the employment of children seems to be an area of the business where managers are particularly effective, at least in the New York and Los Angeles areas. I would assume that the same is true for Chicago.

When one is first entering the business, managers can be very helpful in steering the performer and/or the parent in the right direction concerning pictures, resumes, proper training and set behavior. They also have a pulse on the agents in the area, know the demands of the marketplace and can arrange meetings with various agents and oversee those relationships.

If your child does work in the business, it is your responsibility to make sure the child does not dominate the set. Neither the director, the assistant director, nor the other actors are responsible for parenting your child. If your child 'acts like a child' and is obnoxious from time to time, it is not the responsibility of these people to keep him in line. If he's going to be on the set, he should be on time, attentive, respectful and as focused as possible. (This is why I don't think it's a good idea to make a child conform this much until he is an adult.) He is being paid as an adult and it is extremely rude and unfair to the adults on the set (who are trying to be accommodating, but also have their jobs to attend to) when he is allowed to absorb everyone elses' time and energy.

The only really successful child stars that I have read about are Shirley Temple and Ron Howard. There have been many other successful child *actors* (today Macauly Caulkin is getting several million per picture), but few are able to balance show biz success with a successful *adulthood* beyond the business. Ron Howard's father says that one reason Ron never lost his perspective was that Mr. and Mrs. Howard (both actors) made sure that they never used Ron's money to upgrade their standard of living. As long as they were still supporting Ron and the family, they retained their parental position in the family and Ron was able to stay a little boy. It's pretty hard to come down hard on someone who is paying your rent or who has enough money in his bank account to leave at the first cross word.

For the parent's notebook:

✓ your kid only has one shot at being a kid
✓ your child is paid as an adult, make sure he behaves as one
✓ write for Screen Actors Guild's free pamphlet: "Young Performers Handbook"
✓ know the Child Labor Laws of your state
✓ make your own guidelines if your state has no code or if it doesn't go as far as you think should
✓ don't live on your child's money

- 13 -
Epilogue

By now your notebook is loaded with lots of notes, yours and mine; notes about who you are and where you are going.

Hopefully, you've made a decision to take things as they come. You'll take whatever road is open; acting, directing, producing, casting, etc. and in following these roads, you'll find fulfillment in show business.

You've organized your life, your home, your business space and your way of thinking. You have a specific plan about how you are going to go about making and procuring work for yourself. You now know how to research your marketplace for showbiz jobs of every stripe. You know about agents and unions. You have a support group.

Use all that information. Check your progress. Give yourself monthly and annual progress reports. Remember to celebrate your successes. If you are like the parent who views his child's report card of all A's and one B and only comments on the B, something is going to die inside you.

Success is an inner process *first*. What you *see* *is* what you get. Always *see* the best. Always *see* yourself winning.

Successful people are not procrastinators. Do it now. Do it today.

Good luck. Keep me in mind when you are a big star. I can always use the work.

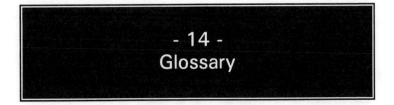
Academy Players Directory - Directory of actors published in Los Angeles by the Academy of Motion Picture Arts and Sciences. Each actor's listing includes one or two pictures plus their agent's name and number. An actor without an agent may list their number or manager's number. You must be a member of one of the actors unions or have a franchised agent to be included in the directory. The Academy Players Directory comes out three times a year and costs $45 for listing in all three issues. The book is used as a reference guide by casting directors, producers and whoever else routinely keep track of actors. Every actor who is ready to book should be in this directory.

Actors Equity Association - commonly referred to as Equity, is the union that covers actors' employment in the theater.

American Federation of Television and Radio Artists - (commonly referred to as AFTRA) covers actors employed in videotape and radio.

Answering services - Answering services come in many forms. The most expensive ones have a tie-in to your phone at home and after a predesignated number of unanswered rings, they will pick up your line. Usually they announce themselves with your phone number or name. They note messages you receive and you call in for that information. The cheaper service has a central number you give to business contacts. They call you there. You call in. The alternative to a service is a good answering machine or *voice mail* where you pay a nominal fee to use someone else's machine. Get something the minute you hit town. Actors simply cannot function without reliable telephone support. There are many excellent services. I have had Actorfone (available in both New York and Los Angeles) for almost 20 years and love them. There are any number of reputable answering services that exclusively represent actors. Check local theater newspapers for ads. Ask your friends about the services they use.

Audition - An opportunity to read for a buyer from your material or theirs, but if it's for a specific project, you will be expected to procure the scene, read and prepare in advance of the audition.

Audition Tape - Also known as a Composite Cassette Tape. A video tape, usually no longer than ten minutes, showcasing either one performance or a montage of scenes of an actor's work. Most agents and casting directors prefer to see tapes of professional appearances only (film or television), but some will look at a tape produced for audition purposes only. Usually on the ¾" U-Matic format although ½" is now being widely used as well. An absolute *must* in Los Angeles market.

Billing - Where your name appears in the credits, the size and how many other people are listed on same line (theater) or card (film or television).

Breakdown Service - Only in New York and Los

Angeles. Started in 1971 by Gary Marsh, the service condenses scripts and lists parts available in films, television and theater. Expensive and available to agents and managers only.

Buyer - Anybody on the road to your future employment. Can be a casting executive, a writer, producer, director or an agent.

Call back - After an initial reading, ranks of auditioners are reduced and the best are 'called back' to read again. Can go on for days.

Cold or Cold Readings - Reading a script aloud with no chance to study ahead of time. *Always* a bad idea. In NY/LA, there are Cold Reading Workshops. I have never understood the value. In my 20-year career, I have rarely been called upon to read a script instantly on first viewing except at commercials where it's a good idea to arrive early, pick up the copy, and head for the bathroom so they won't call you in until you are ready.

Contact Sheets - an 8x10 proof sheet printed by your photographer displaying all the pictures he took of you. Different photographers make different arrangements, but usually the photographer takes at least two rolls of films and you get two different 8x10 prints. The photographer delivers these to you and it is up to you to find an inexpensive place to get these pictures duplicated.

Credits - List of roles the actor has played.

Dailies - Viewing by producers, directors, crew of all

film shot the day before, in order to evaluate perform-ances, lighting, make-up, etc. Actors frequently not allowed to attend.

Equity Waiver - Productions that members of Actors Equity are allowed by the union to work without compensation are called Equity Waiver, Waiver Productions or Showcases. Equity members are allowed to perform as long as the productions conform to certain Equity guidelines, (i.e., limits on the number of performances and seats).

Freelance - Working through many agents at the same time or representing yourself. The bottom line is that you are not signed for representation exclusively with one agent.

Going Out - Auditions or meetings with directors and/or casting directors. These are usually set up by your agent, but have also been set up by very persistent and courageous actors.

Go fer - Term used to describe all-around errand person on a set (or office) who 'goes for' whatever anyone needs (i.e. errands, coffee, etc).

Guesting - Appearing in one or more episodes of a television show. This term is used to differentiate from those actors who are contracted to appear in all or a major portion of the shows.

Hot - Show-biz talk for actor who is currently in great demand.

Industrials or *Industrial Shows* - Splashy Broadway-type musicals produced by and for big business to sell their wares. Pays more than Broadway. Most famous is Monsanto in New York.

Interview - A meeting with a casting director, producer, writer, agent or director. This is different from an audition because in an audition you read for the buyer.

The Leagues - A now-defunct formal collective of prestigious theater schools that offer conservatory training for the actor. The schools still exist, but there is no longer an association. The very best background an actor can have, as far as agents are concerned (other than having your father own a studio). See Reference.

Letter of Termination - A legal document dissolving the contract between actor and agent. If you decide to leave your agent while your current contract is in effect, it is usually possible to do so citing 'paragraph 6' of the SAG Agency Regulations. Paragraph 6 allows either the actor or the agent to terminate the contract if the actor has not worked for more than 15 of the previous 91 days by sending a letter of termination. Also in AFTRA.

> Dear ------:
>
> This is to inform you that relative to Paragraph 6 of the Screen Actors Basic Contract, I am terminating our contract as of ---date---.

Send a copy of the letter to your agent via registered mail, return receipt requested, plus copies to the Screen Actors Guild and all other unions involved.

Retain a copy for your files.

Major Role Performer - Refers to new pay designation in latest Screen Actors Guild contracts that allows no discounts for multiple days.

Mark - term used in rehearsing the camera. You walk through the scene to show the cinematographer and his crew where you will be moving. This movement is determined by the director.

Minimums - Basic union rates for work. See Union Chapter.

Money - Beginning actors work for minimum. As your career progresses, your price goes up relative to your power. Money refers to the largest amount of money you have been paid to date for a day, week, series, etc. See also 'quote'.

Option - Someone pays money to exclusively control a property or a person's services in a particular category for a period of time. Can be followed by a sale or not.

Overexposed - Term used by nervous buyers (producers, networks, casting directors, etc.) indicating an actor has become too recognizable for their tastes. Maybe he just got off a situation comedy and everyone remembers him as a particular character (i.e. Harvard-educated Fred Gwynne as Herman Munster). The buyer doesn't want the public thinking of that instead of his project. A fine line exists between not being recognizable and being overexposed.

Packaging - A large talent agency sells a buyer a *package* including star, director, writer, etc.

Paid Auditions - The practice of rounding up 20 actors and charging them $10 each for the 'privilege' of meeting a casting director. There are agents, casting directors and actors who feel the practice is unethical, but it does give some actors, who would otherwise not be seen, an opportunity to meet and be seen by casting directors. My feeling is that anytime you have to pay to see an agent or casting director, the chances for meaningful employment are slim to none.

Per Diem - Expense money paid to actor for daily expenses above salary. Negotiated by agent. Can include lodging, food, car, etc.

Pictures - The actor's calling card. An 8x10 glossy black-and-white photograph.

Pilot - The first episode of a proposed television series. Produced so the network can determine whether there will be additional episodes. There are many pilots made every year. Few go to series. Of those, fewer stay on the air for more than a single season and most die after two to three episodes.

Players Guide - New York Directory of actors published annually for the New York market. Includes one or two pictures per actor and lists credits and representation. If you work free lance, you can list your name and service. Some list their union affiliation.

Product - For the actor, the product is himself.

Process - People are continually talking about 'the process.' This refers to the ongoing mechanisms involved in developing our personas, careers and/or the rehearsal procedure in a play.

Property - Refers to book, play, story, film that has been acquired for development, production and/or distribution.

Quotes - The most recent negotiated sum an actor was able to command for a particular job. Don't lie. They will check.

Ready to Book - Agent talk for an actor who has been trained and judged mature enough to handle himself well in the audition, not only with material but with the buyers, as well. Frequently refers to an actor whose progress in acting class or theater has been monitored by the agent.

Resumes - The actor's ID. Lists credits, physical description, agent's name and phone contact. See page 123 for a sample lay out.

Right - When someone describes an actor as being 'right' for a part, he is speaking about the essence of an actor (i.e., Paul Newman and Woody Allen will not be seen for the same part.) Also involves credits. The more important the part, the more credits necessary to support being seen.

Roughcut - First piecing together of film. Usually without music, effects, etc.

Scale - See minimums.

Screen Actors Guild - (commonly referred to as SAG) covers actors employed in theatrical motion pictures and all product for television that is filmed.

Seen - Term referring to an actor's having had an interview or audition and being considered for a part.

Sides - Only the pages of script containing your audition material. Usually not enough information to use as source material to do a good audition. If they won't give you a complete script, go early, (or the day before) sit in the office and read it. SAG rules require producers to allow actors access to the script (if it is written).

Submissions or Submit - Agent talk for the act of sending an actor's name to a casting director in hopes of getting the actor an audition or meeting for a part.

Take - Cinematic term used to describe a scene when the camera is rolling.

Talent - Industry-wide term used as a synonym to describe an actor or actors.

The Trades - Show business newspapers. In Los Angeles, Daily Variety and the Hollywood Reporter. Published every business day. They cover all kinds of show business news. Also, Drama-Logue, a weekly of particular interest to newcomers. Lots of information about classes, auditions, castings, etc. All are available at good newsstands or by subscription. In New York, Backstage and Showbusiness. Nationally, the weekly edition of Variety.

Under five - An AFTRA job in which the actor has five or fewer lines. Paid at a specific rate. Less than a principal and more than an extra.

Visible/Visibility - Currently on view in film, theater or television. In this business, it's 'out of sight, out of mind' so *visibility* is very important.

Index

- Exercises -

- Tasks -